Acclaim for

THE EMERGING LAITY

"Throughout our Judeo-Christian history, leadership and authority have taken different forms. . . . The Whiteheads examine these in terms of power and authority pertaining to the Catholic church today. They present an illuminating vision of leadership as returning once again to the grass-roots level of faith community in concert with the present structures of church authority.

The book is scripturally sound, historically accurate, easy to read, and very precise in addressing this issue. It also contains at the end of each chapter a reflective exercise and a list of additional resources for further contemplation and study. It comes highly recommended to anyone serious about ministry in the Church."
— *The Catholic Sun*

"According to the authors, a married theologian/psychologist team, the ministry of the American Catholic Church must respond to a newly emerging vision of the Christian community. That is, it must begin to acknowledge and use the charisma of all individuals, clerical and lay, ordained or not, to meet the needs of the Church here and now. The authors support their challenge by offering historical evidence of evolving patterns and images of leadership, power, and authority dating from Jesus' time. They also present reflective exercises and annotated bibliographies at the end of each chapter to help readers internalize their message. Intelligent, accessible, and stimulating; exceptionally valuable for prayerful pastoral and lay leaders."
— *Library Journal*

"Graciously written, it probes the most sensitive areas of contemporary church controversy without offense, yet challenges all Christians to re-image their notions and practice of membership in the Body of Christ. The comprehensive and annotated references concluding each chapter are particularly valuable. The Whiteheads propose the kind of spirituality requisite if American Catholicism is to have a viable future—smart, lean, and holistic."
— *Commonweal*

BOOKS BY THE WHITEHEADS

The Emerging Laity

Seasons of Strength

Community of Faith

Marrying Well

Method in Ministry

Christian Life Patterns

THE EMERGING LAITY

*Returning Leadership
to the
Community of Faith*

JAMES D. WHITEHEAD
EVELYN EATON WHITEHEAD

COMPLETE AND UNABRIDGED

AN IMAGE BOOK

Doubleday

NEW YORK   LONDON   TORONTO   SYDNEY   AUCKLAND

Image Book edition published in September 1988 by
special arrangement with Doubleday.

Hardcover edition published September 1986 by
Doubleday.

An Image Book
Published by Doubleday, a division of
Bantam Doubleday Dell Publishing Group, Inc.,
666 Fifth Avenue, New York, New York 10103

Image, Doubleday and the portrayal of
a cross intersecting a circle
are trademarks of Doubleday, a division of
Bantam Doubleday Dell Publishing Group, Inc.

Library of Congress Cataloging-in-Publication Data

Whitehead, James D.
THE EMERGING LAITY

1. Lay ministry—Catholic Church.   2. Laity—Catholic
Church   3. Christian leadership—Catholic Church.
4. Catholic Church—Doctrines

I. Whitehead, Evelyn Eaton.   II. Title.
BX1920.W54   1986   262'.15   85-31201
ISBN 0-385-24292-1 (pbk)

BG

We dedicate this book
to the participants, staff and faculty of the

INSTITUTE OF PASTORAL STUDIES
Loyola University of Chicago

a gathering of colleagues,
an assembly of friends

CONTENTS

CONTENTS

ACKNOWLEDGMENTS

This book is about power and leadership, themes that are intellectually complex and emotionally volatile. In bringing the manuscript to completion, we have depended even more than usual on the help of our friends. We welcome this opportunity to acknowledge publicly these generous colleagues.

Patricia Kossmann, our editor at Doubleday, has supported us both by her interest in the book and by the candor of her responses to early drafts. James Zullo, Anne Carr, Sharon Casey, Maria Harris, Robert Kinast and Thomas O'Meara reviewed our initial outline, offering comments that contributed significantly to the final shape of the manuscript.

Virginia Evard, Linda Hayward, Alexis Navarro, Anselm Prior, Trevor Trotter, Mary Ulrich and Sonia Wagner each read drafts of several chapters. Their recommendations were penetrating and helpful; we have incorporated many into our final text. Convinced that a tone of anticlericalism would serve neither this book nor the church, we turned to several friends who are priests for their responses to particular chapters: our thanks to John J. Egan, Frank Kelley, Daniel Dillabough, Joseph Donnelly and John O'Connor for their willingness to help us in this way.

Thomas Sweetser read through the manuscript, in its entirety and on short notice. His perceptive comments have helped us improve both the style and substance of the book. William Thompson and Eugene Ulrich reviewed our discussion of the formation of Scripture in Chapter Nine, contributing to the accuracy of our treatment.

Gordon Myers has been an important mentor in our understanding of groups as systems and our appreciation of the extra-rational dynamics in group life. He served us as a sounding board as we moved the manuscript through a number of drafts. In addition, he gave a detailed critique of several chapters. We are in his debt for all this and much more.

In our relations with these gracious and resourceful colleagues, we have experienced the interplay of power that stands as a core concept in this book. For this, as well as for their invaluable practical assistance, we are grateful.

INTRODUCTION

TWO JOURNEYS

Two journeys have shaped the hearts of our religious ancestors. These were the travels, and travails, of the Exodus and the Exile. For Jews—as for Christians, their spiritual heirs—these journeys hold unending fascination. Historically each happened only once, but they occur again and again in our religious lives.

These are journeys with very different trajectories. The first goes from slavery through a desert to a homeland; the second journey moves from the security of this homeland into exile and then to rescue.

The first passage is really one of invention: a nameless band of ex-slaves, wandering in the hostile environment of the desert, discover their God and their collective identity. In this unlikely climate they are revealed to themselves. It is, in large measure, a journey from absence to fullness: from the emptiness of the desert to the establishment of a nation and a temple.

The second journey pursues a quite different path. Because of their infidelities and injustice, the Israelites found themselves taken from their homeland into captivity in Babylon. Instead of a passage of invention, this was a movement of purification. Dislocation and loss were their lot. God's dwelling place, the grand and sturdy temple, was ruined; their secure life in Jerusalem was replaced by a precarious existence in an alien land. In the midst of this experience of abandonment and grief the Israelites heard prophets urging them to hope. They heard again the promise: once they were purified of their injustice and infidelity, God would lead them home from this exile.

In the Israelites' experience these different journeys called for different kinds of leaders. In the desert their best leaders were clever guides—those able to discern the way, knowing when to travel and when to rest, alert to manna and other nourishment to be found in such hostile terrain. In the new nation with its great temple, their most distinguished leaders were kings and priests, administering the country and the sanctuary. In exile more prophetic leaders were demanded. In this foreign land former kings and priests went unemployed as the people sought leaders who could teach them to both grieve their losses and hope for deliverance anew. Different communities require various leaders: pilgrims look for guides; institutions require administrators; those in crisis need prophets who can help them face the future.

Along each of these journeys idolatry threatened. In their desert trek leaders warned the people against graven images—any artifact that might distract them from their allegiance to an unimaginable God. In exile they found themselves surrounded by idols—the tokens and formulas of alien beliefs. Even amid the peace and orthodoxy of Israel's kingdom and temple, a threat of idolatry endured: the prophet Nathan warned King David that a temple built in splendid triumph could induce the Israelites to forget their origins as a desert people pledged in fidelity to a mobile God (II Samuel 7). If this were to happen, even the sacred temple could become an idol. Further, the very comfort and self-satisfaction of their nation approached a kind of idolatry: a sense of guaranteed righteousness and a growing neglect of the poor tempted Israel toward an ungodly way of life.

Two ancient journeys, shifting styles of leadership, an enduring concern about idolatry: what have these to do with American Catholics today? The fascination of these two journeys lies in their recurrence: they are patterns that we repeat in our private and community lives; these are the routes of our distress and our deliverance. In such passages, even today, we meet God and seek our own purpose.

These images also serve as metaphors for our purposes in this book. In the following pages we hope to trace a purification only just begun in American Catholic life in the past twenty years. We will do this by analyzing the changing interpretations of leadership, power and authority.

The metaphor guiding the reflection in Part One will be that of exile. For many Catholics religious leadership had become exiled, restricted to a small group in the community. To be called to formal leadership was to be called to priesthood; but this vocation was open only to a small part of the community. All the duties of leadership descended on the priest; there was little shared ministry and less mutual accountability. As more educated laity and more assertive women sought to contribute to the community's life of faith, they were calling for the return of leadership from its exile.

A discussion of leadership is always a discussion of power: Who is in charge here? How far does the leader's power extend? But power, like leadership, had drifted into exile. Power had become pictured as a "something" that is possessed by the leader. The priest was understood to "have" the power to say Mass, apart from any consideration of the community. This community celebration had become the sole province of the leader. Thus developed the practice of the "private Mass," a kind of Eucharist-in-exile. To rescue power from exile, we will need to see it not as an individual possession but as a social dynamic. Power is "what goes on" within a community. For Christians this dynamic is stirred, in important part, by the Spirit.

The third exile to be explored in this book is that of authority. The very term suggests a distant, abstract force. We rescue authority from exile when we uncover the process by which communities of faith authorize their hopes and ideals. Authority, returned from exile, is found to be a continual process. Authority is a communal understanding of power: for example, our shared understanding of Scripture and sacraments as authoritative signs of God's power among us. Authority, rooted again in a community's consensus about power, is delivered from its exile as an abstract, unaccountable force.

As the metaphor of exile guides the reflection on community and leadership in Part One, the metaphor of exodus stands behind the schema of Part Two. In these chapters we describe the maturing of Christian life as a cycle of empowerment. This cycle, like the Israelite journey from desert to promised land, begins in a recognition of God's power. We exemplify this stage of the journey for Christianity in the life of Jesus Christ: his recognition and celebration of certain patterns of God's power. The second stage of this journey is a process of authorizing power. As the ancient Israelites gradually authorized their laws and the Torah, Christian communities continued this process of authorization: early generations of Christians selected the canon of Scripture, devised sacramental rites and developed church law. Jesus' prophetic insights about power were institutionalized in the Christian tradition.

This stage of authorizing power, of preserving in institutional form our vision of God's power among us, is a human process guided by the Spirit. As human, it will inevitably entail abuses and failures. Institutional forms tend, ineluctably, toward idols. Laws and structures, once enshrined in social life, become defended for themselves, distracting us from the deeper values they are intended to uphold. This flaw in social life, an aspect of original sin, cannot discourage our development of institutions and laws. We must come to appreciate not the futility of institutions but their continuing need for purification. Here the Israelite experience of exile and the contemporary crisis since Vatican II come together: in a period of purification we are invited to let go ancient and often cherished forms of power and leadership. Prophets appear in the midst of our confusion to help us imagine new styles of leadership and authority.

Seeing and Solving

Our perceptive friend Gordon Myers has instructed us and others on the crucial relationship between seeing a problem and solving it. Seeing precedes solving. Much energy and good will are squandered when, in a time of difficulty or crisis, a group gives its energy to solving the wrong program. We are able to resolve a difficult issue adequately only if we can accurately identify the challenge that it presents.

Consider the "leadership crisis" in the church. The solution here begins in seeing; if we can see the community of faith in a new way, we have new insight into the future of Christian leadership.

A conventional vision of a Christian community saw the group as a collection of individuals in need of various religious services. These services range from marrying to burying, from celebrating to grieving. Leaders are those appointed to see to these needs. The community itself is composed of "children of God," passive and docile before their providing leaders.

Another vision of Christian community is breaking through this stereotype. Here a Christian community is pictured as a center of faith: it is a place where Christ's best hopes shine out—or, at least, flicker attractively now and again. It comprises a group of people who are not only needy but gifted. These gifts appear in all parts of the group: abilities to care for the young and for those who are suffering; talents to manage finances and develop creative liturgies; skills to deal with the complex questions of poverty and social justice. These gifts startle us: they do not arise simply as a result of human calculation. They often seem unaccountable to our planning and beyond our control. They spring from another deeper source that we name the Spirit. These diverse and very practical resources give shape to a group's identity and purpose; clarifying our gifts, we better learn what we are for. And we become more responsible for the group's future.

As we see differently—faith communities as gifted groups of active contributors rather than as passive gatherings of childlike consumers—new solutions to our "leadership crisis" become possible.

This book is about seeing more than solving. We take up some of the concrete questions of leadership in Chapter Five and discuss effective strategies of change in Chapter Eleven. But our larger goal is insight. Catholics today are challenged to see more clearly the nature of the crisis before us so that, together as the whole church, we might envision a response that is adequate to God's future. Our hope here is to serve this new vision, by encouraging more among us to contribute to the task.

In the chapters ahead we attempt to see differently Christian leadership and its two crucial elements—power and authority. If we can see through some of our inherited notions about power and authority, we may more fruitfully imagine both the reality of the Christian community and the service of leadership in its midst.

In this reflection we will be listening to three authorities. Throughout we will attend to our religious heritage about leadership: the images of power, authority and community in the Scriptures and the ongoing wisdom of the Christian tradition. Tradition and Scripture bear a preeminent authority in any Christian reflection, but the Spirit stirs as well in our culture and in contemporary communities of faith. Thus a second authority to be consulted is information drawn from our culture: what might the analyses of leadership and power arising from the social sciences teach us about the shape of Christian communities? The third authority is the current experience of Catholic communities of faith. In the ferment of Catholic life in the 1980s, what hints and clues point the way to the future of leadership among us? To help readers have greater access to the wealth of their own experience on these complex questions of power, authority and leadership, we have included at the end of each chapter an exercise for further reflection. The exercises are designed so that they may be used alone, but their value is often greatly enhanced by sharing with a friend or in a small group setting.

In each of these three authorities we expect to see signs of the Spirit and also to confront evidence of human limitations: in each authoritative source we find God as well as social tendencies to rigidness and idolatry. The confidence that energizes this reflection is that an honest dialogue among these authorities will enkindle both insight and courage. The fruit will be a response that is both faithful and inventive.

Two important notes as we begin. First, our immediate focus in the chapters that follow is the experience of the church in the United States. Parts of this exploration may prove more broadly useful; colleagues in Canada and Australia and England have helped us see important connections between our analysis here and their own experiences. But we are conscious that our discussion of empowerment is set in the American context. The issues, the analysis, the strategies that are relevant in this context will reflect the strengths and limits of this "first-world" experience of personal and social power. The churches of the third world must instruct us about their own journeys of empowerment, travels often taken amid political violence and severe poverty. And in the witness of these courageous assemblies of believers we will all be challenged to a yet more profound understanding of the social dimensions of power.

Second, if—as we shall suggest ahead—"power" is the question in the American church today, "lay people" is not the easy or automatic answer. It is not our contention that the structural purification that confronts the Catholic Church is to be achieved simply by having lay people assume more roles of formal leadership. As those who have worked diligently for the formation of diocesan senates, parish councils and local school boards know, many lay Catholics bring to these roles of leadership images and expectations of power that belong more to the broader culture than they do to the witness of Jesus. A competitive stance toward others, a self-serving attitude toward power, a pride in domination—these temptations of power are familiar to both laity and clergy. As we struggle to devise more adequate forms of shared leadership in the church, we will all find ourselves under the judgment of the gospel.

Finally, a word of gratitude. In 1970 we began teaching at the Institute of Pastoral Studies of Loyola University in Chicago. For nearly two decades this lively community of Christian learning has welcomed and nurtured and challenged us. Here we have been able to test our experience of Christian ministry and leadership in an arena of wise colleagues. In the rich diversity of this community our ideas have been flexed and purified and encouraged. We give thanks to the faculty, staff and participants of the Institute who support us in our own vocation. We salute especially Jerome O'Leary, who first invited us to join him in this worthy effort, and Timothy O'Connell, who continues to model the shared leadership that best nurtures the Christian dream. This mobile community of Christian ministers, gifted and needy, witnesses to us the future of the American church.

PART I

RETURN FROM EXILE

CHAPTER ONE

THE COMMUNITY COMES OF AGE

In the year of our Lord 1960 the Catholic Church in the United States was flourishing. Sunday Masses were filled; Catholic schools were amply staffed; universities and hospitals and social agencies thrived under Catholic auspices. Vocations to the priesthood and the vowed religious life were on the increase. A year earlier the new pope, John XXIII, had announced plans for a worldwide council. This action by the already well-loved pontiff stood for many Americans as a promise of greater flexibility in the church's institutional structure. Moving beyond the insularity and defensiveness of an immigrant church, Catholics had entered the mainstream of American life. Even the President was a Catholic! American Catholics could at last resonate with the imagery and ambition of the early Puritan settlers: this was, indeed, a new promised land.

The mood of the American church in these years was one of confidence. Its vitality seemed to foreshadow a golden age of religious stability and institutional growth. Such was not to be the case. The Second Vatican Council proved to be a watershed. Few among us—the participating bishops included—anticipated the profound and enduring changes that would result from its deliberations and decrees. In the United States the confident enthusiasm of the early 1960s gradually eroded, replaced at first by conflict and then by a growing confusion. But in the midst of the turmoil there were new and unexpected signs of life.

The vigorous movements that had nurtured adult faith before the council—Catholic Action, the Christian Family Movement, Cursillo, Young Catholic Workers—were joined by new efforts: peace and justice networks, Marriage Encounter, base Christian communities. Advocacy groups focused attention on questions of institutional concern: the isolation of divorced and separated Catholics, the inclusion of blacks and Hispanics in the church, the role of the laity, the ordination of women, the development of an effective ministry with gay and lesbian Catholics. Priests' associations and diocesan senates, parish councils and ministry teams were established—many to struggle and even falter—as new structures of collaboration began to emerge. Theology departments in universities and seminaries were staffed by a growing number of American scholars who, trained in the best theological institutions of Europe, were becoming more confident in their examination of the American experience of faith. The American Catholic church—a friendly, youthful giant—was stirring from its "dogmatic slumber." The community of faith was coming of age.

Two long-term but hardly noticed changes had been preparing the church for its coming of age. One was external to the American culture; the other was deeply internal.

Biblical and liturgical research were flowering in Europe after a half century of steady growth. These studies of our shared religious roots were uncovering the experience of liturgy and leadership that flourished among the first generations of Christians. Most of this information was not, of course, available to American Catholics in 1960. But it was available to those preparing for the Council and gradually—through the Council's deliberations and documents—began to influence the local church. This historical research also helped shape the reform of the liturgy through the 1950s and '60s and, in so doing, began a dramatic transformation of Catholic life.

As the results of this historical study were more widely shared, an important realization dawned: our liturgical practice and other religious customs were not eternal! Our current styles of worship and leadership were not identical with those of our earliest religious ancestors. Centuries of pastoral needs and cultural influences had wrought many changes. Three examples may illustrate this discovery, so surprising at the time.

We began to see a startlingly different Eucharist. Among Christians in the first century this liturgy was celebrated more as a communal meal than as a ritual sacrifice. It was celebrated in believers' homes rather than in churches, at tables instead of altars, in the local language rather than in a universally shared tongue. For American Catholics who had become accustomed to the Latin Mass as the "one, orthodox way," this realization would be shocking.

The historical uncovering of the lives of the earliest Christians also revealed a very different world of ministry. Many members of a community participated in this service—preaching the word, caring for those in need, managing the group's resources. Women and men both were active in these ministries. In the first century of Christian life no distinction of clergy and lay had yet emerged; the metaphor of priest was rarely used to describe the community's leaders. In short, the models of ministry displayed in the gospels and the first generations of believers seemed quite novel to us in the early sixties.

Thirdly, these initial communities were actively involved in selecting and evaluating their own leaders. The Christian movement early on lacked the complex organization of an international religious body. Examples are found of local groups electing a bishop and then requesting that he be approved by neighboring bishops through "the laying on of hands." For twentieth-century Catholics, this was a startling discovery. Thus historical research, most of it originating in European centers of scholarship, was a significant impetus to change from "outside" the American Catholic experience.

A second impetus, internal to our cultural life, was the broadening and deepening of the education of American Catholics. For a century and more, most American Catholics had been busy surviving. Immigrants and the offspring of immigrants, they struggled to seize the opportunities this new land promised. Hardworking laity had little leisure and less confidence to give much attention to questions of ministry and leadership. The troubled history of the "lay trustee" experience in some dioceses had made many officials in the American church suspicious of lay initiative. These factors and others contributed to the expectation that lay Catholics should play a more passive role in their parishes than did many of their Protestant neighbors. American Catholics depended, almost totally and often rightly, on the leadership of their bishops and priests.

The generation of Catholics after the Depression and World War II found themselves in a new and privileged world: educational opportunities and greater financial stability gave them the chance to reflect more thoroughly on their religious lives. The laity began to become more involved in what had been the exclusive domain of the clergy. As it had in Europe, the "lay apostolate" developed in the United States as a vehicle of religious formation and Christian action. This new enthusiasm for Christian service still focused the energy of the laity primarily in two directions: Christian witness in the arena of one's work and religious devotion in the context of one's family. Soon, however, the awakening of the laity would lead them to yet another responsibility: greater participation in the life and governance of the community of faith.

These two factors—one internal and one external—came together in the Vatican Council which convened in October 1963. If many American Catholics were unaware of the theological intricacies of this meeting being held in Rome, they could not miss the liturgical changes that the council authorized. Suddenly (it seemed), the altar was turned around; the quiet murmur of Latin was replaced with an almost too familiar English; the Mass, no longer "a private devotion taken together," became a social event. We were allowed to speak during the service, and even encouraged to extend (uncomfortably!) a greeting to the stranger in the next pew.

The disorienting but delightful experience of liturgical change signaled broader developments as well. In the decades immediately before and after Vatican II, visionary priests and religious were encouraging lay Catholics—through both support and challenge—to move into a more mature exercise of faith. Ministry, which had come to be seen as the sole domain of the official leader, was being reimagined as the responsibility of the entire community. Lay Catholics were being drawn beyond a too well learned passivity toward greater responsibility for their own religious lives. Communities were experiencing anew the ancient resources of religious maturity —the adult strengths of conscience and charism.

COMMUNITIES OF CONSCIENCE

Conscience is that personal authority which is the inner guide of Christian life and vocation. While conscience is personal, it is not a private authority. Catholics have long recognized that this inner authority is rooted in communal life. Christian conscience is shaped and seasoned in a community of believers. In a lively community of faith we retell the Scripture stories of hope and conversion and justice. We celebrate God's presence and nourishment in our liturgies. In these ways, in its rituals and through its daily decisions, a community forms the consciences of its members. It is only in such a social milieu (especially in the family and school and parish) that we learn the shape of this inner authority. And it is in these social settings that, over many seasons, our inner authority is tested, purified, refined. Gradually, conscience becomes a reliable resource; it becomes one of the trustworthy voices (along with the other voices of the Spirit in Scripture and church teachings) that guide the complex decisions in which our careers and vocations unfold. This inner authority, developed in community, continues to bind us to one another in our witness of faith. A mature conscience leads not to private compromise or convenience but to mutual accountability and communal discernment.

By the early part of this century, however, these longstanding Catholic convictions about conscience had been muted. After the crisis of the Reformation, Catholic theology seemed to lose interest in conscience—an obviously dangerous (even if essential) source of religious authority. A theology of ministry developed which tended to locate authority almost exclusively in formal structures and designated leaders. Pastoral concern for the development of conscience was overshadowed by a piety that urged increased reliance on the judgments of official leaders. As a result, the inner resource of conscience was ignored and allowed to atrophy. By the time of Vatican II the authority of conscience had become a neglected theme in Catholic life.

As the reforms of Vatican II excited American Catholics to a deeper participation in our faith, these events also quickened our consciences. It became clear that to be called to contribute our giftedness to a community is to be called to be "conscientious"—to develop the trustworthy resources of personal conscience. Without such reliable inner authority, we can participate in community only as children or as victims.

The stress of such an abrupt reawakening of conscience became most evident in the response of the American church to the celebrated 1968 statement prohibiting the use of artificial means of birth control. If this seemed at the time to be a crisis of sexuality, it was more accurately a crisis of authority. Supported by a broad consensus among moral theologians in the United States, a critical number of mature Catholic couples listened to and trusted their own consciences.

This was a new experience among us. Previously, schooled in an attitude of submission on questions of faith and morals, most married Catholics would have quietly obeyed. The few dissenters, unable to comply with official teaching, would have left the church. But since 1968 many married Catholics have chosen instead to dissent and to stay. Experiencing themselves as thoroughly Catholic, they know there is no other place for them to go. Knowing themselves to be responsible both for their family life and for the church, they choose to remain as witnesses to a different view of sexual responsibility. It has been difficult to dismiss these Catholics as irresponsible or to caricature them as sexual profligates. As parents and spouses, they exhibit a seasoned maturity in their lives of faith. In their struggle toward a responsible decision, these couples have consulted their pastors as well as their own experiences. It is through prayer and deliberation that they have come to their conscientious but dissenting judgment.

This response announced the adulthood of the American Catholic church. Pastors and theologians supported married Catholics in following the authority of their well-formed consciences. An earlier docility was being replaced by a hardier virtue of adult obedience. It was an obedience that lived in a community of plural authorities —the gospels, Christian historical practice, church teachings, personal conscience. A livelier if more perplexing faith was being forged.

In our recent past, Catholics sometimes felt themselves confronted with a severe choice between submitting without question to church teachings and following the insights of their own fragile consciences. As we recover the social nature of conscience, its rootedness in communal values, we can begin to heal this unreal dichotomy. Communities of faith (at both the local and the national levels) are shaped by church teachings and, in turn, shape individual consciences. But this is a relationship of mutual influence. These communities, as their own faith matures, witness to the universal church new promptings of the Spirit. Local and regional communities, coming to trust their own seasoned experience of faith, will sometimes instruct the larger church. In Chapter Four we will discuss the authority of this, a community's "sense of faith."

COMMUNITIES AND CHARISM

If the reawakening of conscience was a special gift to the church in the 1960s, a gift of the 1970s was the resurgence of charism. The stirring of conscience drew many Catholics toward fuller participation in the community of faith. But what would be the shape of their participation? This question was resolved in a growing realization of the strengths for ministry among us.

In parishes, for example, where until recently ministry was expected to come exclusively from religious and priests, other women and men began to display a surprising range of abilities. A midlife woman realized (much to her own amazement) that she was very effective in her care for dying persons and their families; a young couple discovered themselves to be good with troubled teenagers; a businessman took it on himself to gather his colleagues for discussion of the ethics of their workplace. Where had people like this been before? They were in our parishes, to be sure. But often their strengths had been hidden from the community, and even from themselves, by expectations that excluded them from any powerful involvement in ministry.

The biblical research that supported the liturgical revolution also helped us name these emerging strengths: we rediscovered the *charisms* in our communities. A charism, in the New Testament as in contemporary life, has three identifying characteristics. It is, first, a personal strength—a particular ability or practical capacity. Whether musical ability or administrative skills, effective teaching or hospitality toward the poor, charism is rooted in "what I do well." Second, charism is a strength that is recognized as a gift. The woman is surprised by her ability to give comfort to those who are terminally ill; the businessman had not always seen himself as the kind of person who could effectively call his peers to a reflection on their professional values. Our charisms call us to be grateful. These abilities strike us as, at the same time, truly ours yet beyond ourselves. We are reminded that they spring not just from our own resources but from the Spirit.

Third, charisms appear in individuals but they are given for the community. They are personal but not private gifts. Charisms appear among us not for purposes of private consolation or piety but to empower our contribution to the group's life. These gifts of care and confrontation, of planning and celebration, bind us in two directions: to the Spirit from whom they come and to the community for which they were given.

After Vatican II, many Catholics began to experience in their own lives the connections between charism and adult faith. To be a mature Christian entails not just needs but gifts. Each of us is gifted with different abilities, whether to challenge or to console or to celebrate. These charisms enable us to contribute to the community as well as to receive from its largesse.

With this realization, Catholics began to recognize charism as a call to ministry. The long-standing distinction between the clergy (as those who minister) and the laity (as religious consumers) began to weaken. Our sense of ministry broadened beyond activities in the sanctuary to include efforts to witness to the gospel of Jesus Christ in the family, the workplace, the world.

Crisis and Vision

The explosion of charism and conscience in the past twenty years is radically altering our understanding of a community of faith. If a parish harbors multiple charisms and many adult consciences, it cannot be a passive object of ministry. More than simply needy, a community of faith is also a source and generator of ministry. It is more than a consumer of programs; it has gifts that are meant to be given away in service. A community is not only a place where

Christian faith is preserved; it is a place from which this faith is to be spread. To believe this is to begin to rethink the official structures of ministry and leadership.

Catholics began to imagine their communities in new metaphors. The inherited image of a hierarchy, with its vertical ranking of different "states of life" (priesthood, vowed religious life, the lay state), had become less compelling. A more horizontal picture of the community began to emerge: we seem to belong alongside one another, rather than above or below. A whole new vocabulary of relationships grew strong among us: collegiality, shared decision-making, team ministry. Enthusiasm for working with one another replaced an earlier reliance on a single leader to provide all the ministries needed in a community.

By the early 1970s these changes were accompanied by a "vocation crisis." Fewer Catholics were entering seminaries and religious orders, while many priests and religious were leaving formal ministry. Amid this decline in the ranks of traditional vocations, new ministries burgeoned among the laity: programs to nurture adult faith, efforts to witness to gospel values in one's work and family life, support networks among those involved in ministries of peace and justice. Many religious and priests who left the formal ministry continued to serve parishes and dioceses as lay persons.

The crisis of vocations appears as a paradox of loss and gain. Some see the crisis as one of generosity; the solution, they suggest, is to urge Catholic parents to instill in their children ideals of greater selflessness and sacrifice. Thus encouraged, perhaps more young Catholics will follow the demanding vocations of priesthood and religious life. To others in the Christian community, the "vocation crisis" seems less a question of generosity than of imagination. The ferment in American parishes today indicates an extraordinary generosity. Busy parents design and staff programs for the religious education of their own and other children; young adults and retired persons commit themselves to a variety of service projects, ranging from diocesan soup kitchens to overseas missionary work; like-to-like ministries develop to support those in crisis—persons widowed or divorced, the unemployed, those seriously ill. More and more Catholics, aroused to their own charisms and consciences, are eager to contribute to Jesus' mission of serving and transforming the world.

A new generosity challenges the existing shape of ministry. The challenge, despite the concerns of some, is not to faith but to structure. Current structures of clerical life and celibacy do not seem able to encompass the new energy for ministry. Can the church imagine new and alternate ways to shape its official roles of ministry and leadership? This is the deeper issue in the vocation crisis today.

To guide its response to such a profound question, the community of faith returns to the life and witness of Jesus. Catholics today prayerfully consult the accounts of the New Testament, not looking for proof texts or expecting to find full and final answers. We seek, rather, to savor the shape of Jesus' leadership. Our hope is that it may serve as our guide in the perilous enterprise of reimagining the Christian community and its leadership.

JESUS ON LEADERSHIP

The life of Jesus Christ, as recounted in the gospels, is a parable of leadership. A forceful and compelling person, Jesus was able to influence crowds but unable to avoid his own traumatic death. Although he was able to touch lives in a healing way, he encountered individuals and groups who successfully blunted his advances. His was a most appealing and often confusing style of leadership. Among his many remarks about leadership, two may serve as an introduction to our exploration of Christian leadership.

The first instruction appears amid Jesus' rejection of certain styles of leadership prevalent in his society (Matthew 23). He denounces the unjust behavior of some Jewish leaders and their pursuit of honors and privilege. Those who ally themselves with Jesus are to practice a kind of community service that has very different titles and a different style:

You, however, must not allow yourselves to be called rabbi, since you have only one Master, and you are all siblings (Matthew 23:8).

Here we follow theologian Elizabeth Fiorenza in translating the traditional "you are all brothers" as "you are all siblings"; this latter phrase expresses the mutuality of their relationship without defeating this very mutuality (for the contemporary reader) by limiting it to one gender.

Matthew's account of this discussion of leadership continues. There are other titles that do not fit the leader who is associated with Jesus:

> You must call no one on earth your father, since you have only one Father and he is in heaven. Nor must you allow yourselves to be called teachers, for you have only one teacher, the Christ. The greatest among you must be your servant (23:9–11).

In these remarks Jesus does not abolish the *service* of teaching and parenting; he disallows their titles as a sign of privilege or excellence. When used to distinguish the leader as holding privileged status, "master, father, teacher" have no place among Christians.

The reason for this disqualification of prestigious titles is at least twofold. These titles distract both the leader and the community from the unique leadership of God, ultimately our sole master, parent and teacher. These titles also position the leader above others, when Christian leaders are properly located on a par with others as their siblings, ready even to humble themselves in acts of service.

In the contemporary world, grown suspicious of the abuses of hierarchical structures, this image of community leaders as siblings and peers, shorn of titles of exclusive privilege, gains new appeal and urgency. Abandoning these titles, we are not left in an amorphous or structureless community. We will always need designated leaders authorized for specific functions in the life of the group. But we need to find names and titles that better designate the service of our leaders, rather than attributing special status to them.

In the second discussion of leadership the mood is one of nervousness and threat. Jesus is leading his friends to Jerusalem, where a confrontation with their enemies is likely. Jesus' disciples "were in a daze and those who followed were apprehensive" (Mark 10:32). Aware that they might soon be deprived of Jesus, James and John approach him to ask for special consideration in the next life. The others, aware that these two might be angling for leadership roles in the group if Jesus should die, grumble and protest. This competitiveness provoked Jesus and he scolded them:

> You know that among the pagans their so-called rulers lord it over them, and their great men make their authority felt. This is not to happen among you (10:42–43).

Jesus points to styles of leadership prevalent in the surrounding culture: governing as "lording it over" or domination; leading as "making one's authority felt." Counter to these cultural modes of leading, Jesus insists on quite another style:

> Anyone who wants to become great among you must be your servant, any one who wants to be first among you must be an attendant to all (10:43–44).

OUT OF EXILE

The theme of this book is the return of leadership to the community of faith. The challenge is to move beyond images that isolate the leader above and apart from the community—in a position of superiority that makes the temptation to dominate difficult to resist. The invitation is to relocate our leaders among the other mature adults in the community. With differing gifts and different roles, we are not all alike. But we are together as sisters and brothers rather than as parents and children or as masters and subjects.

The exile of leadership from the faith community is intimately related to two other dynamics that will be the shared focus of this book: power and authority. When a culture or religious tradition portrays power as an entity that is possessed by individual leaders, it sends power into exile. Power then is imagined and analyzed as though it were separate from the interactions of group life. In this book we will argue for a different view of power. Power refers to all those dynamics that shape the life of a community. Not a possession of some, power is essentially a social process, made visible in the interactions of the different members of the group. The endless challenge of religious living is to distinguish the Spirit-given inter-actions of grace and charism from other, destructive forces in the community. In Chapter Three we explore this social interpretation of power and its influence in Christian life.

When a culture or religious tradition pictures power as an indi-vidual possession, it then defines authority in a similar way. Author-ity is portrayed as "something" attached to certain institutions or roles. This static view of authority exiles it from the interaction and accountability of social life. We will attempt a different approach, in order to bring authority out of exile and into the community. Au-thority, in our definition, is a social interpretation of power. It is what we make of power among us. Communities preserve and en-shrine their best values in certain authoritative places—Scripture, the sacraments, church law. By so doing, the group decides to give these interpretations authority in their shared life. Here the chal-lenge of religious life is continually to clarify and purify these inter-pretations of power. We will examine this challenging image of authority in Chapter Four.

Throughout, our goal is to clarify the community dynamics of leadership. A reexamination of Scriptural images of leadership will assist the effort to locate our leaders more intimately within the community.

REFLECTIVE EXERCISE

In this chapter we have stressed the impact of conscience and char-ism on the experience of American Catholics since Vatican II. We invite you to explore these experiences in your own life of faith. Select a quiet place and time and then prayerfully reflect on these questions.

Recall first an important decision that you had to make in the recent past. Spend some time with the context of the decision—the circumstances, the people involved, the sense of urgency or confu-sion or opportunity that you felt.

In this experience of personal decision-making, how did you ex-perience your own inner authority? To what other authoritative sources did you turn? What was your experience of this "interplay of authorities" as you moved toward a trustworthy decision?

To sense what charism means in your own life, recall a recent experience of yourself as successful or effective, as good at what you do. Be sure to use your own definition of "success" here, looking for the criteria that make the most sense to you. Spend some time with the memory, so that it becomes alive for you.

From this recollection, list three or four of the most significant personal strengths or resources that you see in yourself. Which of these resources do others characteristically call on? What is your own characteristic response to these personal strengths—delight, embarrassment, gratitude? How do these abilities link you to a community that is important to you?

ADDITIONAL RESOURCES

Eugene Kennedy chronicles the changes in the Catholic Church over the past several decades in *The Now and Future Church: The Psychology of Being an American Catholic* (Doubleday, 1984). The National Opinion Research Center in Chicago has been an important locus of systematic research into the contemporary American Catholic experience. In *American Catholics Since the Council* (Thomas More Press, 1985), Andrew Greeley provides a current review of these findings. The new vitality in American Catholic parish life is the focus of a comprehensive study undertaken by the Center for the Study of Contemporary Society at the University of Notre Dame. These findings are being issued in bimonthly reports available through the Notre Dame Study of Catholic Parish Life (Notre Dame, IN 46556).

A difficult but rewarding study of conscience in recent Catholic theology is provided by Richard McCormick in his *Notes on Moral Theology: 1965 through 1980* (University Press of America, 1981). The reader can follow the discussion from the author's observations in the first essay (1965), through the contraception controversy (notes in 1966 through 1968), to his remarks on conscience in 1977 and 1979.

David Power's *Gifts That Differ: Lay Ministries Established and Unestablished* (Pueblo, 1980) gives an excellent analysis of the connections among charism, personal giftedness and Christian ministry. Thomas O'Meara, in Chapter Three of his *Theology of Ministry* (Paulist Press, 1983), offers a clear discussion of charism and its link to service and the upbuilding of community. This book also gives an enlightening overview of how ministry and leadership have changed in different historical periods of Christian history. For a practical theological reflection on the new phenomenon of non-ordained administrator/pastors of Catholic parishes, see Peter Gilmour's *The Emerging Pastor* (Sheed & Ward, 1986).

Another valuable resource is Carolyn Osiek's "Relation of Charism to Rights and Duties in the New Testament Church," in *Official Ministry in a New Age*, edited by James Provost (Canon Law Society of America, 1981). Robert Kinast provides a robust understanding of the participation of lay Catholics in the mission of the church in *Caring for Society: A Theological Interpretation of Lay Ministry* (Thomas More Press, 1985). In a now-classic statement that appeared originally in 1960, John Courteney Murray discusses the theological significance of the American Catholic experience; see his *We Hold These Truths: Catholic Reflections on the American Proposition* (Sheed & Ward, 1960; 1986).

CHAPTER TWO

SCRIPTURAL IMAGES
OF LEADERSHIP

Christian communities recognize God's power among them in their experiences of charism and conscience. As communities of faith are stirred by these religious energies, they become more active and lively. In such a milieu communities begin to reexamine their experience of leadership. In this chapter we will recall the diverse images that are part of the Christian tradition of leadership. We will then attempt to trace the transformations to which these images seem to call us today.

COMMUNITIES AND LEADERS

The expectations we have of our religious leaders are rooted in our vision of God's leadership. Scripture portrays this leadership in three aspects: a transcendent fathering, a filial service and the inspiration of an indwelling spirit. In many of the structures of ministry, however, it is the images of God's leadership as transcendent and parental that have prevailed.

Until quite recently as Catholics, for example, we shared a common expectation about our leaders. These persons were priests, trained and tested in seminaries that were somewhat distant (both geographically and culturally), and appointed to serve the local congregation by church officials. This understanding—that our ministerial leaders are men who come to us from outside the community—has been accepted, even cherished among us. This way of seeing our religious leaders drew much of its strength from scriptural images. Israel portrayed Yahweh as a transcendent Lord: Jesus urged his followers to approach God as a loving Father. These traditions reinforced an awareness of God's presence among us as a powerful ruler and caring parent. Our God, beyond and above human experience, reaches down to comfort and correct us. Our religious leaders were cast in a similar role: capable men, standing somewhat apart from the rest of us, were sent to care for and direct the community of faith.

Our experience of leadership in the community of faith is changing. A new vitality in parishes and schools, in prayer groups and service networks, in ministry teams and religious houses has revealed the extraordinary resources that exist *within* these communities. Leadership has begun to emerge from "unlikely" sources—among the laity, women, those without formal credentials or official roles. Consider these examples.

Scene One. The community of St. John's Parish in the rural Midwest has been without a resident priest for two years. A year ago the bishop asked Bill Masson, an active and widely respected member of St. John's, to handle the practical affairs of the parish between the biweekly visits of a priest. Bill, married and the father of two teenage daughters, was pleased to accept these new responsibilities. Well established in his own small contracting company, he felt it would not be difficult to take the time needed to help out at the parish in this way. After several months of devoting his time exclusively to handling the books and making sure the church buildings were in good repair, Bill was urged by the visiting priest to hold a daily communion service. At these simple prayer gatherings, Bill reads a Scripture passage and distributes the Eucharist that has been consecrated at the biweekly parish liturgy. Recently members of the parish have asked Bill to preach at the daily service—or at least "say a few words" on the Scripture reading. Bill felt complimented by this request but also a little confused. Was this really part of his "job"? Would he be overstepping his responsibilities or meeting the real religious needs of the community?

Scene Two. Sister Ann Ferarra has recently been hired to head the pastoral team of a small Catholic hospital. Her job will be to coordinate the different services offered to the patients and staff of the institution. Ann knows that she will face the same challenge as the leader before her: working with the priest on the staff. Father Grummon sees himself as the only "real minister" on the team, since he alone is ordained. He offers Mass daily in the hospital chapel, distributes communion on the floors and is available to hear confessions. Beyond this, he feels no need for contact with other members of the pastoral staff, in spite of their continual references to "collaborative ministry." Sister Ann wonders: should she give more energy to bringing Father Grummon into the working life of the group, or should the rest of the staff continue to do its best to model a shared ministry, patient with the contradiction in their midst?

Scene Three. Just over a year ago Joan Hulck and Liz Gronowski brought together a number of businesswomen to form a support group. All are Christians, most of them with Catholic background, but with a range of differences among them in terms of formal participation in the church. Feeling doubly marginal in their professions—as women and as committed Christians—they meet regularly for discussion and mutual encouragement. Their conversation ranges from accounts of their personal histories to business triumphs and the usual "horror stories" from the office. These women want to support one another's careers as well as to provide a place to explore the connections between their professional lives and their religious convictions. Recently they have started to include a time for reflection and prayer in these meetings. They find that this moves them quickly to a level of significant sharing. Now that the group has been meeting for several months, Liz and Joan have questions about its religious future. As a group of Christians, where do they belong? Should they seek some affiliation with one of the local parishes? Should they announce themselves to the leadership of the diocese? The group isn't looking for official status or formal recognition: most of the members are even a bit suspicious of official "churchdom"—it seems overwhelmingly clerical and often irrelevant to their own concerns. Yet they sense that it is their common Christian heritage that energizes the group and holds it together.

These examples show us new faces of leadership in the community of faith. In these instances—and the many others that are part of Christian life today—our recent expectations about religious leadership are being questioned, even challenged. Questions arise among us: Who are best able to lead the community into its future? How are our official leaders to be part of the community of faith—as "fathers" or servants, as administrators or prophets? How do the new but unofficial leaders among us fit into our current structures? How will these emerging leaders be nurtured and supported? What part will our established structures have in this revitalization of the ministry of leadership? As we search for answers in a time of change and crisis, we turn again to the riches of the Scriptures: Are there alternate portraits of leadership in these texts? Are there other metaphors of leadership which are a part of our heritage and can illumine our present experience?

Two such metaphors, one in the Hebrew Scriptures and one in the New Testament, arise in our memories today. In them we find intriguing and refreshing nuances of religious leadership.

A mysterious image of God's leadership appears in the Book of Exodus (Chapters 33 and 40) in the story of the "tent of meeting." Wandering in the inhospitable environment of the desert, a disorganized band of nomads—our ancestors—became aware of a compelling presence. A mysterious power moved among them to give direction and purpose to their journey. Our ancestors named this force *Shekinah* or "Presence." This benevolent power was not addressed as a person; it was not imaged as masculine. While utterly beyond the group, this presence did make itself felt among them.

These desert wanderers set up a tent at the edge of their daily encampments as a meeting place with this mysterious power. At a temporary shelter they would await clues about when and where to travel. In the account in the Book of Numbers, the tent of meeting is linked with a cloud that also symbolizes God's mobile presence among them.

Whenever the cloud lifted above the tent the children of Israel broke camp; whenever the cloud halted, there the children of Israel pitched camp.

(Numbers 9:17)

God's presence, imaged in this nonpersonal but forceful metaphor, gave purpose and direction to this group's desert journeys. It showed them the way.

> . . . If the cloud happened to remain only from evening to morning, they set out when it lifted the next morning . . . sometimes it stayed there for two days, a month, or a year; however long the cloud stayed above the tent, the children of Israel remained in camp in the same place, and when it lifted they set out (9:21–22).

God's leadership is portrayed here not in the human metaphor of a patriarch or lord but as a stirring of power within the group itself.

The tradition of an immanent stirring of power appears again in the New Testament account of the Spirit's coming after Jesus' death. Once more the context is absence: now the hostile environment is the time immediately after the community's traumatic loss of its leader. Deprived of Jesus, the first Christian community huddled in an upper room, confused and disoriented. In this domestic desert the Spirit of God stirred. As in the tent of meeting a thousand years earlier, a power began to move *within* the group.

> When Pentecost day came around, they had all met in one room, when suddenly they heard what sounded like a powerful wind from heaven, the noise of which filled the entire house; and something appeared to them that seemed like tongues of fire; these separated and came to rest on the head of each of them. They were all filled with the Holy Spirit. . . . (Acts of the Apostles 2:1–4)

A cloud moving above a desert tent in the Hebrew Scriptures becomes a wind stirring in a room where Jesus is conspicuously absent. This new group of believers, as uncertain as their desert ancestors, are empowered with a new confidence, with gifts of persuasive speech and a sense of direction. The absence of Jesus' leadership, a cause of alarm and trauma for those left behind and apparently deserted, becomes the fruitful context for the disciples' new responsibility and authority. In this emotional wasteland God's power stirs up new leaders—ordinary folk finding themselves gifted in extraordinary ways.

The two scriptural stories portray God's guidance quite differently than our traditional picture of divine leadership. The context is not Yahweh's overwhelming presence at Mount Sinai nor Jesus' immediate presence to his friends; the context is absence. Leadership is imaged not as the action of a particular man but as a wider stirring of power. Finally, leadership is exercised not from above but from within the group itself. The community finds itself empowered with new resources of ministry and leadership.

Many faith communities are undergoing such a transformation today. Some now without official leaders, others experiencing the inadequacy of current structures, these groups find the Spirit stirring among them in gifts and resources that were not recognized before. As these gifts for service are acknowledged, they are given more powerful names: vocation, ministry, leadership. God's guidance is experienced among them not only in the person of an individual leader but as a growing confidence in the group itself. The paradox of poverty (the depletion in the ranks of traditional leaders) and riches (the recognition of new gifts among us) becomes the context for the transformation of religious leadership. The cloud above the tent begins to move; a wind stirs in the upper room; contemporary communities of faith take hesitant steps to follow where this Presence leads.

In the crisis of religious leadership we are rediscovering the guidance of the Holy Spirit. This face of God's care presents a leadership style that is less individual and more communal; that is not limited to males; that is less transcendent (coming from without) and more immanent (arising within the community itself). And we are reminded that the Spirit honors absence. This Spirit stirred originally in the midst of chaos and darkness (Genesis 1:2); it moved again in the absence of the desert; it appeared again in an upper room after the community's loss of Jesus.

When we recover this alternative image of God's leadership we do not deny or overthrow the more traditional metaphors: God as personal leader, as loving Father, as ever present with us. But we do take advantage of the full richness of our religious heritage. Gifted as we are with a tradition rich in images, we tend nevertheless to reduce it to a few, more familiar portraits. We are repeatedly tempted to narrow our vision of religious leadership. The crisis of leadership among us today challenges us to purify our restricted vision and enlarge our hopes for religious leadership.

TWO AGENDA FOR MINISTRY

This fruitful turmoil in the church today suggests two agenda for Christian ministry. The first is to bring the ministry of leadership back into the community. The long history of ministry had led to a separation of official leaders from the practical life of communities. When the priest or bishop was pictured exclusively as the representative of a transcendent God, it made sense to place him above and apart from the community. Rural seminaries, removed from the many distractions of urban life, came to stand as a sharp symbol of the distance between leader and community. Celibacy, gradually experienced less as a personal charism of service than as a legislated requirement of the leadership role, further emphasized the separation of leaders from the community. The expectation that their leaders would be automatically supplied from beyond themselves (coming from the seminaries of dioceses or religious congregations) lulled many parishes into a deep passivity.

Bringing leadership back into the community means establishing programs in parishes to develop and support the diverse charisms of parishioners; it means using a less paternal vocabulary for our leaders; it means being attentive to the new leaders emerging among us, whatever their gender or life-style. The return of the ministry of leadership to the local community does not mean an abandonment of the leader's role as representative of the larger church. It will mean a new and demanding intimacy between leaders and communities.

The first challenge, returning ministry to the community, flows into a second: recognizing leadership as a plural activity in the group. Hierarchical and patriarchal expectations of leadership have led us to picture the leader as singular and even unique: one community, one leader. This has led, over many centuries, to the heroic portrait of the priest as "all things to all men." The diversity of charisms in the community had been absorbed into a single leadership role. The priestly leader was somehow expected to possess every ability of religious leadership—from preaching to financial management, from the care of souls to the development of social programs. If these expectations were tolerable in earlier centuries, they do not match the demands of the larger, more diverse and better-educated parish of today. Both the heightened awareness of the gifts among us and the complexity of group life in the church today argue for plural leaders. But new images are needed to support the collaboration and shared authority required among plural leaders. And new communal strengths and personal virtues will be demanded if these efforts are to succeed.

METAPHORS OF THE CHRISTIAN LEADER

The transformation of leadership now under way in the community of faith will make fundamental demands on us all. Minor adjustments—such as ordaining married men to a permanent diaconate—are not sufficient. Major adjustments—such as allowing women to join a hierarchy of clerical leaders—will not suffice. A reimagining of the Christian community itself is required. The route of this transformation is, as so often in our long religious history, through the desert. We will be invited to desert cherished or at least long-accustomed notions of leadership—as only male, as exclusively clerical, as always to be trained apart from the rest of the community. We will need to see leadership anew—not as a separate status but as an inner dynamic of group life. As is always the case among us as Christians, we turn to Scripture to guide this purification of leadership.

Christian tradition, supported by the culture in which it first flourished, has usually pictured leadership as the activity and responsibility of certain individuals. Four metaphors stand out in this tradition: the leader as king, as father, as servant and as steward.

Each of these metaphors carries certain expectations about community life. Images of leadership never exist in isolation. Each metaphor gives a picture of both the leader and the style of belonging to the group. Each also suggests a particular style of governance: a king's authority, for example, is very different from that of a steward. We will use this review of four traditional metaphors of Christian leadership to trace the connections between leadership and the community.

The Leader as King

The most traditional image of leadership is that of king. The milieu of such a leader is a kingdom or nation, a sociopolitical realm. The metaphor of king suggests both a particular style of governance (ruling by royal decree) and certain ways of belonging to the realm (according to social ranks, ranging from royalty to peasantry). A king has the power to command and rule. Sovereign leaders have power over their subjects and, traditionally, the power to enforce their will.

As monarchy has been replaced by more representative forms of government, Christians have ceased calling their civic leaders "kings." Many wonder how appropriate it is to continue to address God as king. But the move away from kingship as a metaphor of God's leadership invites us to reexamine styles of ecclesiastical leadership as well. We see this in the effort of the bishops of the Second Vatican Council to reenvision papal authority, once modeled on the dominant cultural experience of monarchy, in more collegial fashion. The renewed emphasis on the pope's role as bishop of Rome (a post to which he is elected by his peers) and the reappearance of deliberative synods of bishops are slowly moving Catholics toward a less monarchical and anachronistic vision of religious leadership.

The Leader as Father

Another powerful metaphor of Christian leadership is that of father. Jesus taught us to approach Yahweh in prayer as "our father." Again, this image suggests for Christian groups a certain style of belonging and an expectation about power. The style of belonging is, of course, that of a family; thus parishes and religious congregations often picture themselves as families. The mode of power especially relevant to family life is that of nurturance and instruction. Care and command are blended in the role of the parent—or, more precisely and to the point here, in the role of the father. The parental power of care and instruction may be exercised with gentle respect or with harsh threats. The compelling memories each of us has of his or her own childhood come into play when we use this metaphor, influencing our delight or reluctance around this image of religious leadership.

The style of belonging implied in the family metaphor could, in principle, range from that of the dependent infant to that of the more autonomous adult offspring. But in Christian piety the "child of God" is often depicted as a youngster—someone still lacking a developed conscience or sense of personal vocation. The special peril of such an interpretation is its potential for restraining the believer in religious infancy. The family image can easily lead us to expect a faith community to be composed of a few parental leaders and many dependent and docile children. If we have an image of adult believers, we envision our religious leaders not as caretakers of children but as participants in hardy, mature communities. These mature communities are the meeting places of many vocations and consciences. In such an adult community (a new way of belonging), new modes of leadership and community power will be generated as well.

It should be noted that the images of king and father are both masculine. This is a crucial aspect of our religious heritage. Christianity, developing in patriarchal cultures, borrowed from them gender-specific metaphors of leadership. This borrowing took deep root in Christian ministry: men were understood as "natural leaders" and became the only candidates for ministerial leadership. The metaphor of father, devised by our ancestors to give a provisional shape to a God that we confess to be beyond every name and any gender, gradually came to be interpreted literally: if our divine leader is a masculine parent, then only men can represent him; our priests must necessarily be male. In such a process, suggestive—but partial—metaphors of God's power among us are turned to literal stone; graceful glimpses of God harden into inflexible restrictions. The purification of Christian leadership requires an examination of our metaphors, testing the adequacy of king and father as exclusive descriptions of God and of community leaders.

The Leader as Servant

A third metaphor of Christian leadership is that of servant. This metaphor appears in the moving poetry of the book of Isaiah: the poet describes a beautiful but wounded servant who comes to save a community (52:13ff.). The writers of the Christian gospels saw in such a compelling imagery the portrait of Jesus Christ. Neither a king nor a priest nor a parent, Jesus lived a life of service for others. The story of his washing his friends' feet stands as dramatic witness to Jesus' style of leadership. This paradoxical image of the leader—belonging to a group in a way that differs from being "in charge" and wielding a most peculiar mode of power—has always been compelling for Christians.

The servant occupies the lowest position in the world of rank and status. If the paradoxical delight of this image is its role reversal—the servant/leader is not at the top of society but at its bottom—it still implies a hierarchical world. The strength of the image is that it identifies the leader with the lowly and oppressed. Jesus insists that those who share his values are not to "lord it over" or dominate others (Mark 10:42–44). They are to participate in the community in humbler and more mutual ways. The contemporary limitation of the servant metaphor is its imbeddedness: it belongs to, even while upending, a hierarchical society of "superior" and "inferior."

Another limitation of the metaphor of servant is parallel to that of king: it easily becomes anachronistic and rhetorical. Although service survives as an ideal in contemporary life, the role of "servant" does not. Our memories of slavery and servitude leave little room for this role to be sought out as a religious ideal. And we recall that, as surely as Jesus was neither a king nor a priest, he was neither servant nor slave. He *served* others in a variety of ways but did not occupy the status of servant in any household or group. The image of leader as servant tends to survive chiefly in our rhetoric: government bureaucrats are described as "civil servants" and the pope is called "servant of the servants of God." The survival of this ancient Christian metaphor depends on its transformation: the cultural role of servant must be transposed into the mutual service expected of Christian adults. Service—as a shared expectation, neither restricted to any social class nor exempted in any—will then energize our efforts to care for others as Jesus did.

The Leader as Steward

A fourth metaphor of Christian leadership is that of the steward. This image suffers some of the quaintness of king and servant: the presence of a wine steward, for example, contributes an Old World ambience to a restaurant. Yet this New Testament metaphor holds nuances that may be especially valuable in the contemporary church. "Steward" designates authority without superiority. While responsible for important decisions in a household, the steward is neither a king nor a father, neither a parent nor a political leader. Yet the steward is authoritative in the group, exercising both power and service.

Stewards are responsible for what they do not own. The steward's role combines decisiveness with accountability. In the stewardship image, the power of the leader is real but circumscribed. As we find in Luke's portrait of the good steward (Chapter 12) and in Paul's remarks to the Christians at Corinth (I Corinthians 4:1-5), this kind of leader makes decisions of importance for the household, in the owner's name and in the owner's absence. The steward is emphatically not the owner. Not possessing any ultimate authority, this type of leader helps to interpret the owner's wishes for the community. The steward's authority is thus dependent, a "guest authority." This seems an especially apt description of the leadership to be exercised in the community of faith. The pastor of a parish, the principal of a school, the head of a religious congregation, the director of a project: we fill these roles as "guest authorities"—for a time only, at the pleasure of the Lord. These activities bear an uncanny resemblance to the decisions with which all adult Christians—whether parents or political figures, bishops or business leaders—find themselves confronted daily.

The nuances of stewardship in the Christian Scriptures merit further scrutiny. "Steward" is an Anglo-Saxon translation of the Greek word *oikonomos*—one who sees to the law *(nomos)* of the household *(oikos)*. Stewards are thus those persons who oversee the domestic order—the rhythms and rules and compromises by which a household or community thrives.

The word "steward" appears in the gospels only in Luke's account, and then only at two points. The first appearance is in the famous parable of the faithful steward (Chapter 12). This story highlights three features of the community leader. First, such a person acts as a servant rather than as a master. Second, the chief virtue of a steward is a combination of wisdom and trustworthiness—an experienced dependability. Third, the context of this service is absence: the leader makes responsible decisions in the absence of the master or owner. Many community questions demand resolution in such an uneasy period; the steward is called to exercise a provisional authority in such circumstances.

The second appearance of the steward in Luke's gospel is in the story of the unjust steward who, about to be fired, is astute enough to reduce the accounts of his master's debtors (Chapter 16). Again the steward acts with a certain wisdom or shrewdness; the steward also acts on his own authority and in the absence of the master. St. Paul, in his first letter to the Corinthians, repeats these characteristics of the steward: such a person functions as a servant; must be a trustworthy individual; and performs in the absence of the master "until the Lord comes" (I Corinthians 4:1–5).

Its precarious position as authoritative service is meant to deprive stewardship of independence and possessiveness. The virtue of trustworthiness points to a reliability, an inner authority that has developed "on the job" and on which both the steward and the community can depend. Such an adult strength looks very much like a well-seasoned Christian conscience: an inner authority and sense of faith guide contemporary stewards in their contributions to the community.

The third characteristic of stewardship is more complex and frightening: the context of such service is absence. The authority of stewards arises both from their trustworthiness and from the absence of their masters. This absence compels the steward to a more authoritative role in the group.

For the earliest Christians, it was an experience of absence that provoked their own stewardship. After Jesus' death the first communities felt the absence of his leadership. As we recalled earlier, this traumatic loss brought forth some startling results: it was Jesus' absence that created the space for the Spirit to appear among these Christians on Pentecost. This ancient power—the saving power of Yahweh, experienced so compellingly in Jesus Christ—appeared anew in the physical absence of Jesus. As long as the Lord was among them, the first disciples had only to follow: they had only to pursue the guidance of their powerful leader. When the Lord is present, we are all fittingly disciples.

But in the "generous absence" created by Jesus' death a leadership vacuum was generated. The disciples' typical question—"How do we do it around here?"—would no more be answered by a physically present Jesus. Now, seasoned and experienced community members would have to answer the disciples' question. The power of the Spirit, stirring in the absence of Jesus, invited disciples to become stewards.

It is unsettling to speak of Jesus' absence. To be sure, the Lord was not utterly absent. Because of his continued presence in the Spirit, we remain a community of disciples. But this is not a physical presence that can be experienced in a single leader knowing God's will for this group. It is a mysterious, spiritual presence to be attended to and uncovered in a community's prayer and decisions. It is a presence that is affirmed and safeguarded by the authoritative actions of a community's stewards. If we really believe in the Lord's ascension (his departure from us) and his second coming (his promised return), we must believe in Jesus' absence now. And we must learn to honor that absence. We honor his absence by refusing to burden our leaders with the demand that they provide us with unambiguous answers or protect us from the demands of change. Our participation in the leadership of our communities is another of the significant ways by which we honor the Lord's generous absence.

In our book *Seasons of Strength* we offer a developmental interpretation of Christian stewardship, locating its authority in the maturity of an adult vocation and conscience. To raise a Christian family is itself a challenging stewardship; to instigate a faith-sharing group among one's business associates is an exercise of stewardship; to organize a gathering of divorced Christians demands the confidence of a steward; a parish council succeeds best when understood as a gathering of the community's stewards.

Another advantage of the metaphor of steward is that, like servant, it is not gender-specific. One need not be a man to qualify as steward. Each mature Christian is invited to stewardship: the maturing of our vocation and conscience makes us more reliable and trustworthy; our discipleship is seasoned until we are able to contribute, authoritatively, to the life of our community. As co-stewards with other mature Christians, we become able to share the responsibility of our generation of believers to hand on the faith to the future.

IMPLICATIONS FOR CHRISTIAN LEADERSHIP

Each of these four metaphors, deeply rooted in our religious tradition, interprets leadership in individual terms: leadership is pictured as a characteristic of a single person. In the following chapters we will explore an expanded view: leadership as a dynamic of group life, a dynamic that can be neither understood nor exercised apart from the social interaction of a community. Before turning to this exploration we can draw several implications for leadership in the Christian church.

The first concerns the variety of the metaphors for leadership in the New Testament. The Scriptures provide us with no one absolute model of leadership. Instead we find here a rich variety of images. Our own stewardship invites us to let go metaphors which have become less persuasive, such as those of king and father. We need not reject or abandon these metaphors; but we open ourselves to the revelation found in other, presently more compelling images —such as the authoritative service of stewardship.

As we celebrate anew the ancient metaphor of stewardship, two additional implications become clear. There is a need to recover the connections between this style of leadership and adult faith. We do not do well to isolate stewardship in certain high-profile positions such as those of bishop or pastor or principal. All Christians are called to the special, if partial, authority of their consciences. We are meant to be, finally, a community of stewards. This demands a shared leadership and a recognition of leadership as a dynamic of the group's life, rather than as a possession of an individual leader.

The other implication to be drawn from our reflection on stewardship concerns absence. Because absence is so often experienced as negative and painful, we tend to avoid it and even to disguise its appearance among us. But the New Testament calls us to an acknowledgment and even celebration of absence. Examples of absence as graceful are abundant: the parish without a pastor learns to be more creative and aware of its gifts; a team loses its leader and discovers, in that absence, new resources and potential; leaders, when they can absent themselves from a need for total control, find powerful new abilities that had been hidden. The Spirit appears to love absence. As we acknowledge absence, we create space for the Spirit to stir new possibilities for our shared life of faith.

REFLECTIVE EXERCISE

In a reflective mood, return to an image of leadership in Scripture that is significant for you—an event in Jesus' life, a story from the Old Testament, a passage from one of the letters to the early communities of faith.

Let this image or story become present to you. Take time to dwell in it, recalling the elements of the story or the meaning of the passage. Be aware, as well, of the thoughts and feelings that the image calls out in you.

After this time of presence, take some notes of what this image suggests to you about the shape of Christian leadership. Be as concrete as you can; try to name the elements and ingredients that are important, as you see it.

Consider the styles of leadership you experience in the church today—your own style as well as those of other persons in leadership roles. In what ways does the scriptural image upon which you have been reflecting *support* these experiences of leadership? In what ways are these styles of leadership *challenged* by the scriptural image?

You may wish to bring this consideration to a close by reading prayerfully the scriptural passage upon which you have been reflecting.

ADDITIONAL RESOURCES

The tent of visitation, in its earliest form, was a place where God *appears* rather than dwells (Exodus 33:7–11; 40:36–38). This "portable sanctuary" was eventually enshrined in the temple in Jerusalem. For a brief overview of this history, see Xavier Léon-Dufour's *Dictionary of Biblical Theology* (Crossroad Books, 1977), p. 594, or Bernard Anderson's *Understanding the Old Testament* (Prentice-Hall, 1975, 3rd edition), pp. 104 and 182. Both scholars note Israel's hesitance about "institutionalizing" God's presence in the temple. The prophet Nathan objected most fiercely to King David's plans, arguing that such a stationary sanctuary would lead Israel to forget its time in the desert and its instruction about God's mobility: "I have never stayed in a house from the day I brought the Israelites out of Egypt until today, but have always led a wanderer's life in a tent" (II Samuel 7:6).

An excellent resource on the history of Christian leadership is Edward Schillebeeckx's *Ministry: Leadership in the Community of Jesus Christ* (Crossroad Books, 1981). The eminent Dutch theologian continues his exploration of the contemporary challenges of leadership in *The Church with a Human Face* (Crossroad Books, 1985). Karl Rahner analyzes the role of the community leader, in his typically complex but fruitful fashion, in "Pastoral Ministries and Community Leadership," in *Theological Investigations, XIX* (Crossroad Books, 1983), pp. 73–86.

Elizabeth Schüssler Fiorenza provides a difficult but rewarding analysis of the influence of patriarchy on the shape of Christian leadership in *In Memory of Her* (Crossroad Books, 1983). The contemporary translation of stewardship is pursued at greater length in our chapter on "Stewardship: The Disciple Becomes a Leader," in *Alternate Futures of Worship: Christian Leadership* (Liturgical Press, 1987), edited by Michael Cowan.

CHAPTER THREE

COMMUNITIES AND POWER

"Stir up your power, O Lord, and come." This Advent prayer is being answered among us today as Christian communities experience God's power in charism and conscience. As these groups mature, they confront the central questions of religious power: Where is God's power among us? How are we to act as stewards of this power? In what ways does the gospel shape the institutional structures of power in the church? Christian communities mature as they respond faithfully to these stirrings of God's power among them.

THE AMBIGUITY OF POWER

As Christians, we have learned to be cautious of power. Reluctant to become involved with power ourselves, we have been suspicious of those among us eager to take it up. Schooled to be "meek and humble of heart," we have depicted Jesus more as a gentle comforter than as a confrontational prophet. But today, with the help of biblical scholarship, we are recognizing that power is everywhere in the New Testament. The most common word for power, *dynamis* (its root survives in the words "dynamic" and "dynamite"), appears more than a hundred times in the New Testament. At times it even serves as God's name: Jesus, raised to glory after his death, will be "seated at the right hand of Power" (Matthew 26:64).

Jesus' life is intimately involved with power. He confronts the destructive power that has reduced the possessed youth to a near beast. He touches eyes that are blind and ears that are deaf and empowers them to sight and sound. Approached by a sick woman in the midst of a crowd, Jesus pauses: "I felt power flowing out of me" (Luke 8:47). And, in passages that can strike us as strange, he encounters situations that defeat his powerful interaction with others. When a group near his hometown refuses to believe, "he could do no miracles there . . . he was amazed at their lack of faith" (Mark 6:5–6).

Whether in the life of Jesus or in our own experience, power remains ambiguous. We confront this ambiguity first as we attempt to define power. Often there is a temptation to think of power as a "thing," as a packet of energy that forceful people carry about. In our ordinary speech, for instance, we say that someone "has" power. Like money, power seems to be a substance that can be accumulated, hoarded or squandered. To picture power in this way —as an entity—also settles the question of its location. Power resides within individuals, as a personal possession.

An alternate image of power is gaining influence today. We are beginning to recognize power as a *relationship* rather than as an individual possession. Power refers to interactions that go on among us. It describes the energy with which we attract each other and bind ourselves in mutual commitment. It also describes our efforts to restrain and coerce others in unhealthy and destructive relationships. Power is best perceived not as a private strength but as those interactions that both create and threaten human community.

The New Testament word for power *(dynamis)* supports this interpretation: power is a *dynamic*. This image of power gives a new perspective on its location: power is not something that leaders carry about with them; it is a process occurring *within* a group. To "locate" power in this way, in the group's interaction, radically influences the role and status of leaders.

These two images—one, which sees power as "belonging" to leaders, and the other, which sees it as the interaction of the group —alternate in the New Testament accounts of power. One tradition, recorded in Chapter 9 of Luke's gospel, remembers that Jesus "called the Twelve together and gave them power and authority over all devils and to cure diseases, and he sent them out to proclaim the kingdom of God and to heal" (9:1–2). God's power is pictured here as something that Jesus "has." As leader of the community, he gives this power to the Twelve—a select group of leaders. The power of leadership passes from Jesus to individual leaders rather than to the community as such. The understanding of an individual "succession of power" from Jesus to Peter to the present pope finds its roots here.

A very different tradition emerges from the final chapter of Luke. Here Jesus appears to his followers after his death, encouraging them to "stay in the city then, until you are clothed with the power from on high" (24:49). Here the community, not individual leaders, is the focus of Jesus' concern. It is a disoriented group, deprived of the empowering presence of Jesus. His appearance foretells the reemergence of power among them. They will soon be rescued from the loss of power which they experienced in his death; they will be "clothed with the power from on high."

According to this tradition, expanded in the Acts of the Apostles (2:1–4), the first community of Christians huddles in an upper room, impotent after the death of their beloved leader. In the midst of absence and loss, this group receives the power of the Spirit. God's power stirs in the group, taking tangible form in a variety of gifts and in a new collective confidence.

The first tradition, recorded in Chapter 9 of Luke, portrays power as the possession of leaders and suggests a continuity of power through the community's loss of Jesus. It bridges the gap between the death of Jesus and the emergence of ministers and leaders in the earliest communities. But, in bridging this real crisis, it tends to disguise it. This celebration in Luke of God's enduring power among us has been especially welcomed at times in our institutional history when we have needed to reinforce the continuity of apostolic succession.

The second tradition portrays power as the dynamic interaction of Jesus and his followers and, following Jesus' death, the interaction of the Spirit and the group. But this tradition more boldly acknowledges Jesus' death as disruption, as a paralyzing loss of power in the life of his followers. The resurrection announces the survival and triumph of God's power in Christ. But the announcement comes first in a scattered way—to the women at the tomb, to the apostles, to the two disciples on the road to Emmaus. With the coming of the Spirit at Pentecost, the church celebrates the emphatic return of power to all the members of the community. By both acknowledging the disruption of power and celebrating its reemergence, this tradition can help illumine the crisis of religious leadership today.

POWER AS A SOCIAL PROCESS

In the social sciences, too, the image of power as a process is growing in importance. In his far-reaching analysis of political leadership, historian James McGregor Burns notes

> that power is first of all a *relationship* and not merely an entity to be passed around like a baton or hand grenade; that it involves the *intention* or *purpose* of both power holder and power recipient; and hence it is *collective,* not merely the behavior of one person (*Leadership,* p. 13).

Social analyst Elizabeth Janeway, whose work we examine in greater detail in Chapter Eleven, makes the point even more succinctly: "Power is fundamentally a relationship between people."

We can look to the parish setting to illustrate these relationships of power. In a thriving parish social power tends to be diffused. The community is aware that its resources are spread widely among its members. The sense of participation is high. Many people, for example, are involved in preparing the Sunday liturgy—the priest-celebrants, the musicians, the lectors, the ministers of communion, the hospitality committee who serve coffee and doughnuts after each Mass. An active parish council supports and questions the pastor and professional ministry staff. The social justice committee challenges a budget decision, urging that parish funds be designated to support a sister parish in the inner city rather than to renovate the parish hall. The youth group lobbies for a more active role in parish deliberations. A loosely organized group of parishioners, feeling left out, resists any movement of change—thus contributing its share to this interplay of power.

When we examine this parish we see its power—the actions of cooperation and compromise, of conflict and challenge, that characterize this community of faith. In the everyday, practical interplay of this group's life, power is not confined to the behavior of only a designated few. Power *emerges* in the relationships that develop in the parish. This is what it means to say that social power is a process more than a possession. Social power flows in the group; social power *is* the flow of collaboration and resistance and debate through which these people interact with one another.

Power, then, is essentially social. To understand social power we must look at relationships—at what goes on among people rather than at individuals alone. As members of the community interact, power flows in many directions. As power stirs in a group, its members begin to shape this energy into patterns and rules that give order to their common life.

Christians recognize the energy flow among them, the surprising and continued stimulus to pursue their best hopes and ideals, as the power of the Spirit. It is in these interactions of generosity and forgiveness that we have our most practical experiences of grace. These are the relationships that show us God in our midst. This power is not possessed only by the group's official leader or ministers; it moves and stirs among the different strengths and hopes that constitute this community.

The power of the Spirit in the group moves among other forces alive among us—envy, compulsion, resentment, competition. A Christian community is continually challenged to discern and distinguish the Spirit's power from these other, destructive energies. The power of the Spirit is a dynamic that binds the group to the values of the gospels. It is to preserve and hand on these values that communities organize themselves by developing structures and roles.

Structures of Social Power

In this discussion we are stressing a new image of power. We are urging that power be examined not as an entity—as though it were "something" that a leader possesses—but as a process that goes on among us. But it is easy to lose sight of the *process* involved in power. The robust interplay of our lives together can be masked by the social structures that develop. These social structures can both foster and frustrate the group's power.

In any group over time, predictable patterns begin to emerge—"this is how we do it around here." What we expect of one another becomes more settled; how we act toward one another becomes more predictable. We begin to define a structure, that is, the regular ways that the group's work will be shared. We select leaders and set out rules of procedure. Through offices and procedures we say "out loud" our understanding of how power should flow among us.

These structures develop as members come to expect different things from one another. Sociologists see this as a process of *role differentiation*. Roles appear in a group as we face the practical question, Who does what? Again, let's take an example in the parish. A number of single adults come together informally to share their frustration at feeling marginal to the family-oriented activities at St. Agatha's Parish. After an hour or so of lively conversation they decide to meet again in the hope that some common action can be planned. As the group looks to this next meeting, they consider how to share some tasks. After some discussion it is settled: Helen will meet with the parish staff to tell them of the group's concern; Jack will bring the soup and bread for the simple meal that will precede the meeting; Mary will prepare the prayer service for its close.

Two aspects of this first stage of role differentiation are worth noting. This is an *ad hoc* designating of roles: we are deciding these tasks only for next week. The group, as yet, has no history or any pre-established roles to guide it. (Its members may, of course, carry a considerable legacy of cultural expectations: "Is it wise to have a woman make first contact with the pastor? Why is a man preparing the food?") Secondly, these designated roles are closely related to natural abilities. Jack enjoys baking and cooking; Helen is skillful in communication and negotiation; Mary is comfortable with public prayer. This *ad hoc* determination of the flow of power for next week's meeting is expectably close to the contributors' charisms: they are good at what they are assigned to do.

A second stage of role differentiation happens as tasks are repeated and patterns begin to emerge. Mary assumes responsibility for much of the group's prayer life; Jack regularly supplies the food;

Helen can be expected to handle difficult negotiations. The other group members are aware that these persons do a good job. We are coming to expect them to give these services and they even seem to enjoy it. The amorphous flow of power in the group is being shaped into specific patterns of reliable strengths. The three roles, accepted by the other members of this group, give a good order to its fledgling existence.

A third stage of role differentiation develops as these patterns of behavior are further stabilized into definite structures. The group decides to appoint Mary formally to plan the group's prayer over the coming year; Jack is designated head of the food committee; Helen is asked to be the group's ordinary liaison with the staff and other groups in the parish. With these formal designations and the establishment of a term (for the next year), the group has evolved the structure of "office." Notices go out; titles are discussed; office space is sought out. *Ad hoc* roles have developed into patterns of reliable action and then into structures of power.

The impulse to develop an explicit power structure is often commendable. Setting up standard procedures can save time and effort. Having determined ahead of time "how we do it around here," we can proceed quickly and confidently. Both the advantage and the danger of the established power structure are that it "regularizes" the flow of power in the group. In some situations this serves the group well: individuals know what is expected, time is not wasted in repeated negotiation about recurrent tasks, the group's talent and experience can be tapped to put the best person in the right position. But such a regularized flow of power, for all its convenience, is likely to distract us from new energies and potentials appearing in the group. Knowing too well the established patterns of power, we may neglect other stirrings in the group.

We need to remind ourselves constantly that every power structure is a *human artifact*. For the good order of our group we have assigned special importance to certain roles and offices. We have established a certain priority in the patterns of power among us. Organizational charts and job descriptions give these patterns greater visibility. The advantage to the group of developing these structures is clear. The danger in this process should be equally obvious: this attempt to "locate" power in offices and lines of procedure easily masks the dynamic and fluid interplay of power that is the group's life. The influence of the office holder, thus objectified, easily becomes separated from the group. Power is seen, then, to *belong* to this office and these procedures. These structures, now declared sacred and unchangeable, become idols of power. This danger becomes fully visible in the next stage of role differentiation. In this next stage we leave Helen, Jack and Mary as we trace the roles and offices that have emerged in the group from their initial contributions.

In the fourth stage these roles and offices become enshrined as the exclusive and privileged structures of power in the group. Now *only* the person in charge of the liturgy can make decisions about it; *no one* except the head of the food committee shall see to this area of the group's life. Power comes to be pictured not as a group dynamic but as a possession of the leadership role. The office now carries its own independent power, which is conferred on the person who moves into this job. Whoever occupies this office has the right to perform its duties—whether gifted for this role or not, whether accepted by the community or not. And since it is the office that gives power, *only* the officeholder can provide this service. Everyone else "lacks" the power. Office tends to be pictured as the *automatic* and *exclusive* source of power in the group. The necessary tension between the powers of charism (personal giftedness) and office (formal designation) is strained to the breaking point. The leader, now fully empowered by office and role, can survive the absence of personal ability and even of community approval.

Power in Relation

As we seek to organize our lives in groups, we necessarily establish patterns and then structures of power. This is the unavoidable but perilous process of objectifying power. We "objectify" when we turn our interactions into an *object*—a stable, fixed thing. We objectify power when we treat the group's strength (which is, in fact, diffused throughout the members and expressed in the messy give-and-take of their relationships) as though it were "located" primarily in some smaller focus of the group's life—a particular leader, a designated role, a set of established rules. Such objectification is, as we have said before, a normal and necessary part of every group's life. The effort to clarify roles helps us come to some agreement about what it means for us to be together as a group. Developing a power structure gives us a common understanding of how our group can accomplish its tasks. Defining "leaders" and "followers" —distinguishing between those in priority roles and those in subordinate positions—sets out our understanding of how the group's resources can best be organized for the common good.

The problem is not that these distinctions are made but that we begin to treat these distinctions as *permanent* and *privileged*. Permanent: functional distinctions begin to be treated as essential differences. Not only do our leaders have different functions in the life of the group; they themselves *are* different. The power differences among us become rigid and fixed. The conviction grows that leaders and followers cannot change places, since "leaders are not like the rest of us." Privileged: functional distinctions start to be linked to differences in status. When this happens, being in the leadership role brings with it other benefits—title or prestige or wealth. Gradually these benefits are seen not as linked to the leader's special service to the group but as personal privileges. A conviction grows that leaders have a *right* to "more" than the rest of us.

The recognition of power as a social process does not require that the structures of group life be abolished—but that they be recognized as *relative*. Structural differences among us are relative, first, because they exist *in relation* to the larger goals of the group. It is to serve these goals better that we accept the distinction between leader and subordinate, realizing—as we do—that we are objectifying a fluid process of interaction into a formal structure.

The distinction between leaders and followers is also relative in that it is limited in its scope. The distinction applies, properly, to agreed-upon differences between us in regard to *certain areas* of our life together. As a nation, we agree that the person elected as President will take precedence in the processes of national decision-making in a number of stipulated areas over the next four years. As a religious congregation, we agree that those who function in roles of congregational leadership are legitimate interpreters of our communal vision and we recognize our bond of obedience with them while they function in these offices. As members of an organization, we understand that roles of designated leadership are established for the common good and we acknowledge the specific authority of those who function in these roles.

In each of these cases, the structural distinction is real but limited. The structure points to differences in power that exist in a particular context—the life of *this* group, the management of *this* project, the achievement of *these* goals. When it is thus, structure serves the larger good of the group. It is when these real but limited distinctions between leader and follower become *absolute* among us, when these contextual "differences" in power are generalized into a permanent dichotomy between the strong and the weak, that structure becomes destructive.

In reality, social power functions through the mutual interaction of the group's members. Structures, when they become rigid and nonnegotiable, effectively mask this interdependence. The leadership role then loses its reality as a working distinction and becomes an autonomous state. Those in leadership roles begin to be understood as *being* different, rather than as exercising different functions. As this happens, leadership is separated out from the inconveniences of group interaction and gradually begins to exist apart from the challenges of mutual accountability. Power becomes a "thing" that can be possessed. The social reality of power, as a process that goes on among us, is disguised.

We will explore further this complex process of social power in Part Two. In the final section of this chapter we will examine one of the ways in which the church is recovering its sense of power as a dynamic in the community.

THE CHURCH AS SACRAMENT

In the church and in particular communities of faith God's power stirs, moving us to believe, celebrate, seek forgiveness and do justice. This continual stirring of power is more than simply rhetorical. It takes tangible shape in a group's recognition of its purpose and its surprising ability to celebrate even loss and death. Concretely, we tend to identify this power in its particular manifestations: in the variety of charisms—preaching, healing, challenging—found among the group's members. To nurture and orchestrate this flow of God's power in the community we establish roles and offices of leadership. As we have just seen, these efforts to channel the Spirit's power among us, necessary and useful as they are, also carry with them severe temptations. We can come to identify God's power as *belonging* to these roles, as located exclusively in our leaders. We thus face the ever present need to purify our structures: to remind ourselves that the power of the Spirit is not bound by our institutional forms but moves through the church for its own transformation and for the healing of the world.

In the deliberations of the Second Vatican Council the bishops reaffirmed—even if somewhat cautiously—the social nature of Christian power. Near the beginning of the Document on the Church *(Lumen Gentium)* we read: ". . . the Church is a kind of sacrament. . . ." The authors display some hesitance in this observation: they note that the church is *a kind* of sacrament and then hasten to add a footnote explaining that the word "sacrament" is applied to the church "by analogy with the seven sacraments." The church is judged to be a "general sacrament" because it is where the seven sacraments are celebrated.

This hesitant statement marks a transformation in Catholic thinking about the sacraments. For a very long time these powerful rituals of healing and celebration were envisioned as individual actions of the ministerial leader. The priest (alone) had the power to celebrate the Eucharist and to forgive sins. The individualized power of the sacraments was emphasized in the anomaly of "the private Mass" and in baptism performed apart from community participation.

Over the centuries the sacraments had come to be seen as specific rituals that only official ministers were empowered to perform. This led to a fascination with the "matter and form" of these rituals: a concentration on the exact words and precise gestures that constituted the sacramental formulas. An almost obsessive attention to the celebrant's behavior distracted the church from the community's participation in these saving actions. A reversal of this individualized vision of the sacraments is under way in the church today. We are recognizing (following the tentative suggestion in the Vatican II document) that the church itself, and particular communities of faith, *are* the sacrament of Christ in the world. Christ's presence—his hopes and values and mission—become palpable and believable in the daily activities of dioceses and parishes, ministry networks and other groups of Christians. Each maturing group of believers *is* a sacrament: "Where two or three meet in my name, I shall be there with them" (Matthew 18:20). The sacraments are the basic power structure of a Christian community.

A community's practical actions of celebration, reconciliation and justice announce Christ's presence in the world. These repeated, communal actions testify that life is not meaningless, that competition and self-defense are not our only stance in regard to our neighbor. These actions witness to God's benevolent presence among all of us—a presence from which we are so easily distracted. Because it acts sacramentally, a community *becomes* a sacrament—an enduring sign of grace in the malaise of human affairs. The ritual celebrations of the sacraments are rooted in and are expressions of this sacramental character of the group. In a group that does not believe in God's presence, the sacrament of the Eucharist celebrated by a priest will be experienced as an empty ritual. Among a group that is unable to forgive, the rite of reconciliation can only be seen as an ineffective gesture. As theologian David Power has suggested in "Liturgy and Empowerment," the vitality of the individual sacraments depends on the community's practical and daily exercises of faith, forgiveness and celebration.

Catholics continue to recognize the communal features of these rituals once seen as (simply) priestly actions. Vocabulary changes: "the community celebrates the Eucharist" replaces "the priest says Mass." Rituals change: in the Rite of Christian Initiation of Adults (RCIA), the community assumes a much more visible and active role in the baptism of its new members. Matrimony is recognized not as a private affair between couple and priest but as a public act of faith in which the couple formally assume a new mode of contribution within a community of faith.

This return to the more ancient vision of the community as the basic sacrament radically adjusts the sacramental role of the leader. This official role is one of orchestration, giving order to these communal activities and reminding the group of its holiness. No longer pictured as the uniquely empowered person who *brings* the sacraments to an expectant but passive community, the leader is now envisioned as the coordinator and presider in the sacramental life of the group. As coordinator, the leader orchestrates the various efforts of celebration, forgiveness and healing always going on in the community. As presider, the leader is commissioned to keep these sacramental activities faithful to the larger sacramental tradition of the church. The leader thus reviews new efforts and oversees celebrations, without necessarily having to lead the community every time it gathers for prayer.

The presider is also called to represent to the larger church the grace and insight of this community's particular sacramental experience. Thus a special significance of this position of community leadership is its contribution to both an internal order (coordinating this community's different gifts and needs) and an external order (strengthening its relationship with the larger church).

The revolutionary insight stated so hesitantly in the Vatican II document is that each faith community *is* a sacrament. The power of the sacraments cannot be restricted to leadership offices or specific rituals. Nor is this power of celebrating God's presence among us simply imported to communities by formal leaders. Such a view exiles the sacraments in particular rituals and separates leaders from the community. In truth, the sacramental power of the Spirit is constitutive of every group of maturing Christians. The group's believing, forgiving and healing *are* themselves sacramental. When we acknowledge this we welcome the sacraments' return from exile. And we are encouraged to purify the offices and structures of leadership that serve the sacramental group.

REFLECTIVE EXERCISE

For many of us, power remains ambiguous or even negative. Take some moments here to explore your own awareness of power. Begin with an exercise of centering, to clear your mind and focus your concentration.

Close your eyes. Take a deep breath, exhaling slowly; repeat this several times. Then slowly count backward from the number ten. As you count, let each number become visible in your imagination. Hear the number sound in your imagination as well. When you reach zero, remain quiet for a moment or so.

With your eyes closed, let the word "power" arise in your imagination. See the letters of the word take shape before you; hear the word sound in your mind. Be attentive to the word, present to you in this way.

Then let your own images of power arise. Don't force an association; just remain receptive to whatever image comes. It may be a picture or a song title, a visual memory or a mood. Spend several minutes with the image that comes, letting it develop as it will. If more than one image arises, spend time with each.

Finally, take some notes about the images of power that arose in your reflection. What do these images suggest about your own awareness of power?

ADDITIONAL RESOURCES

Theological discussions of power continue to exhibit a deep ambivalence about this aspect of Christian life. In *Christ and Power* (Fortress Press, 1977), theologian Martin Hengel is hesitant about Jesus' power to excite and stir crowds (see, for example, p. 21). As the title of his book—*Church: Charism and Power* (Crossroad Books, 1985)—suggests, Latin American theologian Leonard Boff is influenced by the traditional dichotomy of charism and structure. At times this dichotomy is expressed in the text as well, as in his description of the first generations of Christians: "this Church is free of power" (p. 50). Here power is assigned an exclusively negative and institutional meaning—a decision that strands charism "outside" the discussion of power.

Theologian Walter Wink has begun a detailed study of power in the New Testament. In his first volume, *Naming the Powers* (Fortress Press, 1984), he analyzes the vocabulary of power in the New Testament, stressing its use in the plural sense—"the principalities and powers." Wink translates these strange forces not as disembodied spirits or angels but as the inner and outer aspects of human institutions (see especially pp. 5 and 104). As the outer aspect, they are the visible structures and laws of an organization; as the inner aspect, they are the spirituality or driving force of the same institutions.

James McGregor Burns's analysis in *Leadership* (Harper & Row, 1978) has become a classic in the interpretation of effective political governance. Elizabeth Janeway's discussion of the relational quality of social power comes in her wide-ranging review of theory and research findings in *Powers of the Weak* (Knopf, 1981). In "Power and Authority in Organized Religion" *(Sociological Analysis,* in press) Richard Schoenherr distinguishes two movements of social power in necessary tension in religious groups.

Janet O. Hagberg provides an intriguing look at the "stages of personal power in organizations" in her very readable book *Real Power* (Winston Press, 1984). In *Women, Men, and the Psychology of Power* (Prentice-Hall, 1981), Hilary M. Lips analyzes the place of power in relationships between women and men.

Theologian Bernard Loomer discusses power from the perspective of process theology in "Two Kinds of Power," *Criterion* (Winter, 1976). For a practical look at the dynamics of power in contemporary ministry, see Roy Oswald's *Power Analysis of a Congregation* and John C. Harris' *Stress, Power and the Ministry,* both available through the Alban Institute (Mount St. Albans, Washington, D.C.) *Power and Authority* (Christian Brothers National Office, 1976) presents a series of papers dealing with these dimensions in the context of vowed religious life.

For the section on the church as sacrament in the Vatican II document, see *The Documents of Vatican II,* edited by Walter M. Abbott (America Press, 1966), p. 15. For an excellent overview of a practical and communal view of the sacraments, see Tad Guzie's *The Book of Sacramental Basics* (Paulist Press, 1981). David Power's discussion of "Liturgy and Empowerment" is found in *Alternate Futures of Worship: Christian Leadership* (Liturgical Press, 1987), edited by Michael Cowan.

CHAPTER FOUR

COMMUNITIES AND AUTHORITY

Power generates community and community generates authority. The power of Christian values—forgiveness, celebration, justice—draws us into lives of mutual commitment. In our communities we preserve and institutionalize these values: we give them authority in our lives.

In a Christian community we link the growing authority of our personal vocation with the authoritative structures of this group's life. We commit ourselves to its goals and procedures; we join forces with other members and with those designated as its leaders. Such a commitment ushers us into a world of plural authorities. This world is not static, with rules and roles that are finally fixed; it is mobile, open to development and purification. As our own hopes and values are strengthened by and contribute to a group's vitality, we become participants in its power and active preservers of its authority.

Authority is not "something" uniquely possessed by our leaders and our laws. It is, instead, a continual process of protecting and purifying our deepest hopes and values. This is a community event to which every believing adult is invited. As we appreciate the dynamics of the authorizing process, our communities are enlivened and our leaders are rescued from exile.

THE EXILE OF AUTHORITY

Early in the sixth century before the Christian Era, the nation of Israel, defeated by its enemies, was led into exile in Babylon. In exile the people lived under foreign powers and alien authorities. Israel found itself in a new desert—its temple lost and its homeland abandoned. For a generation they endured as strangers in a strange land. As confusion gave way to despair, prophets arose—like Ezechiel—and began to stir hope of rescue from this exile. In the book of Deuteronomy we find an account of God calling the Israelites back from this bondage. Summoning them to courage for the return home, Yahweh instructs the people where they are to find their authority:

> For this law that I enjoin on you today is not beyond your strength or beyond your reach. It is not in heaven, so that you need to wonder, "who will go up to heaven for us and bring it down to us, so that we may hear it and keep it?" Nor is it beyond the seas, so that you need to wonder, "who will cross the seas for us and bring it back to us, so that we may hear it and keep it?" No, the word is very near to you, it is in your mouth and in your heart for your observance. (Deuteronomy 30:11–14.)

The authority of God's word was not in exile in some distant place; it is within their own hearts. A recovery of their own authority required not permission from a distant power but a communal introspection. Having lived so long in exile from their own authority, our religious ancestors needed to be coaxed back to it. Christians today find themselves involved in a similar return from exile.

For many Christian communities authority has become alien and distant. As a people we have come to envision authority as something that originates outside of our own lives. Authority seems to reside in certain places and people: police have authority and federal statute books are repositories of authority. So, too, bishops exercise authority and canon law is authoritative among us. Many Christians have come to the conclusion that a basic feature of authority is that it dwells beyond them. If our only image of authority is as a force that comes from the "outside," then authority—however benign—becomes external. And as our history shows us, authority that is seen solely as external soon becomes authority in exile.

The exile of authority experienced in many communities today has been influenced by two historical developments. At the beginning of the fourth century the Christian church underwent an extraordinary transformation. When the Emperor Constantine became Christian, Christianity moved from its status as a countercultural religious movement to become the official religion of the Roman Empire. The church, still relatively small and loosely organized, started to model its structure on the political design of the Empire. The leaders of the Christian community were soon recognized as composing a distinct social class—the clergy. This new status separated these leaders from ordinary, "lay" Christians. The structure of dioceses appeared, as bishops, who had previously been local pastors, became regional administrators. This organizational development had ministerial consequences, moving bishops away from direct pastoral work.

Buoyed up by this new societal recognition, the church continued to be influenced by its cultural environment. Bishops began to be called princes of the church. As titles of excellence multiplied, the image of the leader as servant of the community became overshadowed. Increasingly, ecclesiastical leaders came to be seen as an independent group and their ministerial ties with particular communities of faith became further obscured. The clergy's difference in social rank was soon reinforced by the adoption of distinctive clothing. A difference in life-style appeared, as celibacy became a requirement for ordination to priestly leadership. Leaders were becoming separated from the community, taking authority with them.

A second portentous change in Christian leadership occurred in the eleventh century, in the reforms of Pope Gregory VII. The pontiff sought to extricate the church and its leaders from the political machinations of various national powers. The Christian church, the pope argued, is different from other groups; it is an autonomous reality founded by God and answerable only to God. He urged that his religious authority be acknowledged as absolute. Begun as a separation of the church's authority from that of other political powers, this movement succeeded in severing the papal leader's authority from the Christian community itself. As absolute, the pope's authority was accountable to *no* human group—including even communities of faith. Authority—that participatory process of preserving a group's values in laws and institutions—went into exile in the independent office of an absolute leader.

One bitter fruit of these historical events, as Yves Congar and other theologians have observed, was a novel understanding of "the church." Gradually, discussions of the church became examinations of its hierarchical structure of leadership. "The church" came to refer not to the whole body of believers but, instead, only to its institutional arm, its official leadership.

A second painful consequence of these developments was the atrophying of the authority of personal conscience. If *all* authority resides in the administrative arm of the body Christian (we do not say "head," since Christ is the head), the authoritative contributions of the other members of the body are depreciated. If our leaders know, comprehensively and unerringly, God's will for us, there is no need for the authority of a personal conscience. Consistently ignored, the strength of personal conscience began to wither.

Protestant reformers in the sixteenth century reasserted the importance of personal conscience and its authority. Church leaders, reacting against this challenge to ecclesiastical control, further diminished the role of conscience. As a result, among many Catholics a childlike reliance on the external authority of official leaders came to replace the hardier, adult scrutiny needed to form and trust the inner authority of conscience.

The gradual and sometimes painful recovery of the authority of personal conscience is part of a larger ferment in today's church. We are experiencing a return of authority from exile. The journey is from an exclusive vision of authority as an immutable force "out there" toward a renewed appreciation of the continuing process of authorizing by which a religious community lives its faith.

AUTHORITY AS AN INTERPRETATION OF POWER

In his book *Authority,* social psychologist Richard Sennett provides a careful and evocative analysis of this communal process. Authority or, better, the process of authorizing includes two essential elements. Authority refers to the understanding of power that is both *explicit* and *legitimate* among us.

Sometimes a group's understanding of power remains implicit: we have a general sense of "who does what around here" and that seems to be all we need. But often our convictions about social power—about how initiative and influence should be exercised among us—are expressed more explicitly. We state them in our laws and constitutions; we make them visible in the formal roles and standard procedures through which we organize our life together. This is the first ingredient of authority: it is an *explicit* understanding of how social power functions among us.

But it is the second ingredient—legitimacy—that *creates* authority. A group's decisions about power are to some degree conditional, that is, dependent on circumstances, subject to controversy, based on certain assumptions. As Americans, for example, we govern ourselves as a constitutional democracy rather than as a monarchy. As Christians and Jews, we use "covenant" as the ruling metaphor of our life with God rather than another image. As Catholics, we recognize *these* books as part of sacred Scripture, excluding others. In each of these examples, choices have been made which now carry authority in our lives. When we see these decisions in historical perspective, we recognize that different choices could have been made. Things could have been otherwise. But the choices that were made now exert influence in our lives; we accept them as legitimate. Legitimacy means that what "could have been otherwise" has been accepted as natural and necessary.

Authority, then, refers to patterns of social power that are both explicit and legitimate: *explicit* in that members are generally aware that this is how things *do* operate in the group; *legitimate* in that members generally acknowledge that this is how things *should* operate in the group.

This process of attributing authority to certain roles and particular rules is a necessary part of social life: without it our values do not survive and our commitments know no boundaries. But there are risks. The biggest risk is that after assigning authority to roles and rules we may lose sight of our part in the process. As this happens, authority—like power—begins to be understood as something "out there," with a reality apart from our contribution. This is the route by which authority journeys into exile.

Our language fosters this tendency to objectify authority, to treat it as a "thing." We speak of authority as "belonging to" a particular person or as "invested in" a certain role. But authority is not a thing: it is an *interpretation*. Authority is the explicit *understanding* of power that stands behind and supports the everyday structures of the group's life, those regular patterns that shape relationships among members.

Among Christians, this communal interpretation of power is rooted in Scripture and the sacraments: these are the authorized channels through which we understand God's power to flow among us. In Chapter Nine we will trace the historical process in which earlier generations of Christians have authorized these two structures of power.

Authority, then, is the explicit face of social power in a group. To "have" authority means to be acknowledged as having the right to be heard and heeded, the right to make demands on others. But authority is not self-justifying. Born out of the group's decisions about power, authority looks beyond itself for legitimacy. Ultimately we acknowledge a pattern of social power as "authoritative" among us—as having the right to our allegiance and compliance—because it serves the deepest values of the group. This larger good which grounds the legitimacy of authority has been expressed in different images: philosophers, for example, speak of the "common good"; social analysts refer to the "goals of the group." For Christians, the larger good that grounds the legitimacy of authority is twofold: the coming of the Kingdom of God in charity and justice, and the upbuilding of the church in order to serve that essential goal. Patterns of social power (such as the directives for selecting new bishops or for establishing pastoral councils) become authoritative for the community of faith through their connections with these larger purposes. And, as we shall see in Chapters Nine and Ten, these patterns remain authoritative only as long as there is consensus that they serve the larger purposes of the group's life.

Authority, then, is an act of interpretation; it is what we make of the power among us. To define authority as an interpretation of power is not to suggest that it is simply arbitrary or subjective. Christians do not invent God's power. But we do generate images of God and structures of religious life that give this power a particular historical shape. This process of "authorizing power" is precisely how a religious tradition comes into existence. In the late first century, for example, Christians evolved the leadership roles of elder (presbyter) and overseer (bishop): these designated leaders were authorized to guide the communities' life. The history of Christian ministry is, in part, the continuing interpretation of these roles of authoritative service. The ferment in today's church often centers on our efforts to authorize structures of leadership and service that respond to new invitations of the Spirit.

Christians as Authorizers

When we stress that authority is an interpretation of power, we remind ourselves that we are participants in that process. We do not just "discover" the patterns of authority that we shall live by; nor did they simply appear, magically, among the first Christians at Pentecost. In prayer and debate our ancestors constructed the earliest authoritative structures of community and ministry. We are called to be partners in this continuing process of acknowledging and safeguarding God's power among us and determining what uses of power are legitimate. We may be silent partners, reinforcing by our passivity a pattern that we distrust. Or we may become active in the struggle to develop patterns more responsive to the community's deepest values. But we are always participants, involved in the interplay that reaffirms or challenges the current shape of Christian authority.

Two examples of the communal process of authorizing patterns of God's power, one ancient and one contemporary, may clarify this dynamic so central to Christian faith. The four gospels are the most authoritative texts for those who call themselves Christians. A static, ahistorical view of Christianity would have us see these four books as divinely produced apart from the messy process of human editing. A more realistic view acknowledges these texts as generated by different communities in response to the Spirit's inspiration. These texts hold God's revelation for us, but this is a revelation interpreted and authorized by human communities.

The fourth gospel provides an excellent example of this historical process of authorizing, even within the sacred texts. Written some twenty years or more after the three earlier texts of Mark, Matthew and Luke, it is quite different from its antecedents. This gospel was composed in a cultural setting that held new concerns and cherished unique imagery. In place of Matthew's and Luke's stories of Jesus' infancy, we find the bold announcement of an eternal Word become flesh. We are introduced, for the first time, to the stark imagery of light and darkness: "a light that shines in the dark, a light that darkness could not overpower" (John 1:5); "I am the light of the world!" (8:12). The earlier gospels' recollection of Jesus' anguish in the garden of olives is nowhere to be found in this narrative.

What is the fourth gospel doing? Why is it veering from the "orthodox" approach of the three already completed accounts of Jesus' life? The fourth gospel authorizes an interpretation of God's power in novel imagery; it is attempting to make the life of Jesus Christ compelling in a different cultural context. In his studies of the Joannine community, theologian Raymond Brown has explored the group struggles and communal hopes that generated this extraordinary text. This process—authorizing new interpretations of God's power—that we find in the fourth gospel is one in which contemporary Christians continue to be involved.

For many of us, our own more humble participation in this authorizing can be glimpsed in our everyday efforts to hand on our faith to our children. We choose particular passages from Scripture to read with them. By selecting these stories among many, we *authorize* them—often implicitly but emphatically nonetheless. Our decision to recall *this* story gives it greater authority in our children's lives. We may choose, for example, to tell our children stories that emphasize the goodness of their bodies, or we may prefer to neglect these accounts. Whichever we do, we authorize for them certain interpretations of power: our silence about sexuality reinforces their confusion and shame as surely as our respectful discussion authorizes their growing comfort with their changing and sometimes mysterious bodies. Similarly, when we talk with our children about the difficulties and demands of justice, we authorize again the gospel insistence on our responsibility for our neighbor. If we fail to show a concern for justice, our silence authorizes the neglect of this central Christian value. Justice is a power that survives in Christian life only as we continue to authorize its pursuit.

Adult Christian life is itself an ongoing process of authorization: our actions either preserve and authorize the hopes of Jesus or legitimize their neglect. As adults, we cannot escape this responsibility. When we cling to practices that seem orthodox (even if obsolete), we authorize the stagnancy that results. When we work toward a new vision of community and ministry, we offer the modest authority of our lives to these larger hopes.

Authority, we are arguing, is neither static nor is it isolated in our leaders. Authorizing is a community process in which every maturing believer participates. When we recognize our responsibility in this communal process we rescue authority from exile. In this adult stance the faith community looks to its leaders not to "deliver" authority but to orchestrate and order the authorizing process to which charism and conscience call us all.

AN AUTHORITATIVE SENSE OF FAITH

The return of authority to the community of faith is being fostered today by the recovery of an ancient Catholic conviction: a Christian community, as it matures, is expected to develop a "sense of the faithful."

The sense of the faith is an internal source of the communal authority that is crucial to a group's religious maturing. It is a seasoned and tested sense of how *this* community is to live its faith—to do justice, to celebrate the Lord's presence, to witness to forgiveness. The Document on the Church *(Lumen Gentium)* in Vatican II recognized this special characteristic of a faith community:

Thanks to a supernatural *sense of the faith* which characterizes the People as a whole, it manifests this unerring quality when, "from the bishops down to the last member of the laity," it shows universal agreement in matters of faith and morals. [Our emphasis.]

The sense of faith is a consensus. It is a confident intuition proper to the body of believers. Cardinal Newman, writing in the middle of the last century, described the sense of faith "as a sort of instinct . . . deep in the bosom of the mystical body." Concretely, this sense of faith is the church's intuition about particular aspects of its life—its need to care for the poor and disadvantaged, its conviction about the holiness of human love, its insight about the shape of Christian ministry.

Cardinal Newman argued that it is this community instinct about the faith that *preserves* and *protects* Christian belief. It preserves the faith in times when the church's official leaders are neglectful of their vocations. Despite these failures in leadership (the Renaissance popes are a dramatic example of such a lapse), the faith endures, instinctively and viscerally, in the other members of the body. Abuses regularly sweep through the church, but the faith survives—grounded as it is in the well-seasoned instincts of many faith communities. This sense is, finally, a surer guarantor of the faith than is doctrinal subtlety or charismatic leadership.

This community intuition, according to Newman, also protects Christian belief from error. Mature communities have a sense of what actions are genuinely Christian. There exists, in Newman's words, "a jealousy of error, which it at once feels as a scandal."

In the Vatican II document which rescued the notion from a historical amnesia, the sense of faith is described as a universal, global consensus. In the 1980 synod of bishops, devoted to marriage and the family, a more practical nuance appeared. In the resolutions of the synod the bishops urged that the teaching church *learn from* the life experience of married Christians. This suggestion, both obvious and surprising, admits that married Christians carry in their bodies—physical and social—a maturing sense of how Christian marriage is to be lived. This is a religious instinct not available to an unmarried leadership and from which it is to be instructed.

But this development at the synod of bishops pointed to an even more important implication of a living "sense of faith." The intuition of faith, if it is genuinely and practically rooted in the religious experience of different communities, will not always speak in a single voice. We see that the sense of faith will, at times, diverge from standard practice and conventional statements of belief. For example, it was an increasing sense of the value of communication in the vernacular that led to recent liturgical reforms. Similarly, a maturing sense of "lay" participation in ministry is altering the structure of Christian service in many dioceses. A changing awareness of women in many communities of faith today questions their exclusion from official leadership in the church.

When we restrict the sense of the faithful to a universal and rhetorical level, we avoid these messy problems. But if we accept the reality of the "sense of the faithful" in the practical life of the community of faith, we must confront our diversity. This will be a scandal only if we are committed to an immobile and ahistorical uniformity in faith.

When we acknowledge that the sense of faith of a community is its collective conscience, we recognize that it will be both universal and specific. It will be in union with the tradition, since its formation as a *Christian* conscience binds it to its heritage; but it will also, at times, come into tension with some of this tradition's conventional expressions. Without such a vital diversity, uniformity gives way to stagnation, canceling any effort of purification.

A community's specific sense of faith is the core of its corporate vocation. A community is more than the sum of its individuals' vocations. Any group of Christians, as it matures, develops a sense of purpose, a desire to express its faith in concrete, specific ways. Its vocation and its conscience take shape; it is beginning to express its sense of faith.

As we more clearly identify the intuition of faith that is characteristic of any maturing community, we also recognize that this seasoned set of instincts is the source of the group's authority. If a group has no sense of vocation or purpose, it will lack any sense of religious authority. If a Christian parish, or school, or family sees itself exclusively in passive and dependent images, it will develop no authority. It will wait to be authorized, again and again, by other more authoritative members of the body of Christ.

The authority that grows as a group's sense of faith is seasoned has two sources. The dependable authority of *this* community grows from its years of faithful discipleship to the gospel, its years of fidelity to the demands of Christian values as interpreted by the ongoing tradition and articulated by its official leaders. And this authority is also rooted in the group's intimate and immediate relationship with the Spirit. The Spirit of God, dwelling in any genuine and maturing community of faith, constantly stirs such a group with insights, charisms and courage. This Spirit authorizes the group to actively express its faith. We recognize the authenticity of the Spirit in this group when its actions are both faithful to its shared past and prophetic of a purified future.

In a severely hierarchical vision of the church, the Spirit is mediated to a faith community exclusively by its official ministers. These leaders both bring the Spirit, in their sacramental ministry, and judge the authenticity of its stirrings. In such a vision, the community can only *receive* its sense of faith, never participating in its active formation. Exiled from any participation in authority, the group must wait to be authorized before acting. Such a passive sense of faith will never generate a collective conscience or community vocation.

A rigid vision of authority would restrict this sense of faith to its universal and unchanging expressions. But if we acknowledge that authority is, in fact, a process of authorizing, we see how different communities participate in this collaborative effort. Purification and reform happen as particular communities, seasoned in the faith and authorized by the Spirit, challenge those parts of Christian practice that have become ungraceful. Recognizing that the process of authorizing Christian life is a shared venture, these communities are aware that their insights do not comprise the whole of Christian faith. Such groups do not "leave" the tradition or repudiate those communities whose experiences of faith differ from their own. Instead they witness—sometimes patiently, sometimes truculently—to the intuitions of faith that they sense to be authentic. It is such maturing communities of faith among us today who argue, authoritatively, for a less restrictive structure to ministry, for a less elite understanding of the priesthood, for a more trusting embrace of human sexuality.

Communities of faith are coming alive today in a renewed sense of their vocation and conscience. They are listening, carefully, to discern their own special instincts of faith—about justice, or sexuality, or celebration. As they listen, and learn to trust these instincts, they become more authoritative in the faith. And they remember that this authority comes from the Spirit and is an authority shared with other, different communities.

The continual and arduous authorizing of Christian life is a coauthorship: in partnership with the Spirit, our official leaders and other communities, we celebrate and preserve our deepest values. Neither children of convention nor victims of structure, our seasoned communities share authoritatively in the mission of handing on the faith to the next generation.

REFLECTIVE EXERCISE

Authority, as an abstract noun, is difficult to comprehend. To come to a more concrete sense of its reality in our lives, we invite you to the following exercise.

After a few moments of quieting yourself and maintaining a meditative mood, ask yourself this question: "What is the most authoritative thing I have ever done?"

Let arise whatever comes—an important decision, a confrontation, an interior resolution. Try to recall the various elements of this event: How did it happen? What persons were involved in it or affected by it? What was the outcome? How did this authoritative event affect your sense of yourself?

If possible, share this reflection with others. Compare notes: What are the similarities among your experiences? How is your own experience unique or special?

ADDITIONAL RESOURCES

For an overview of the history of Christian authority, see Yves Congar's excellent and brief "The Historical Development of Authority in the Church: Points for Christian Reflection," in *Problems of Authority,* edited by John M. Todd (Helicon: 1962).

John L. McKenzie's influential book *Authority in the Church* (Sheed & Ward, 1966; 1986), so provocative when it appeared in the 1960s, remains an important statement today.

Richard Sennett's analysis of the social process of authorizing power is found in his *Authority* (Vintage Books, 1981). Robert A. Nisbet discusses the intellectual history of authority as one of the "unit-ideas" in sociology in *The Sociological Tradition* (Basic Books, 1967).

See Raymond Brown's discussion of the conflicts and consensus that contributed to the fourth gospel in his *The Community of the Beloved Disciple* (Paulist Press, 1979). For a fuller exploration of the sense of the faithful, especially as rooted in the seasoned instincts of adult faith, see Chapter 12, "Ministering to the Sense of the Faithful," in our *Community of Faith* (Winston-Seabury, 1982). Cardinal Newman's discussion of this instinct can be found in *On Consulting the Faithful in Matters of Doctrine* (Sheed & Ward, 1961, 1986). Leonard Swidler examines the pluralism and dissent that are essential elements of a "sense of faith" in his "Demo-Kratia, The Rule of the People of God, or Consensus Fidelium," in *Authority in the Church and the Schillebeeckx Case,* edited by Leonard Swidler and Piet Fransen (Crossroad Books, 1982).

The practical dynamics of authority in the local parish setting are under discussion in two useful pamphlets available through the Alban Institute (Mount St. Albans, Washington, D.C.): *The Mystery of Clergy Authority,* by Cecilia A. Hahn and James R. Adams, and *The Authority of the Laity,* by Verna J. Dozier. We take up the interplay of "Authority and Obedience" in Chapter Twelve of our book *Seasons of Strength* (Doubleday Image, 1986).

CHAPTER FIVE

AN EMERGING PORTRAIT OF LEADERSHIP

Christians today are reenvisioning power and authority, seeing these not as abstract entities but as dynamics of group life. Power arises in the interplay of our differing strengths and needs; authority is the continuing process of emphasizing our most valued patterns of power—such as those we experience in Scripture and in the sacraments. As power and authority are thus lured out of exile and reinserted within the community, we are brought to reimagine leadership. In this chapter we will trace the interpretation of leadership as an inner dynamic of the community's life.

ORDERING THE BODY

The earliest Christians described themselves as "the body of Christ." St. Paul seems to have taken special pleasure in this metaphor of intimacy and interdependence. In his letter to the Christian community in Corinth he elaborates the analogy between a faith community and a body:

> Just as a human body, though it is made up of many parts, is a single unit because all these parts, though many, make one body, so it is with Christ . . . (I Corinthians 12:12).

This complicated interplay of different powers describes both a human body and a body of believers:

Now you together are Christ's body; but each of you is a different part of it. (12:27)

For Paul, this was more than a pious image; the metaphor suggests the energetic challenge of body building:

If we live by truth and in love, we shall grow in all ways into Christ, who is the head, by whom the whole body is fitted and joined together, every joint adding its own strength, for each separate part to work according to its function. So the body grows until it has built itself up, in love (Ephesians 4:15–16).

The earliest Christians believed that Jesus, absent after his death and ascension, was still present among them. In a true sense, these communities were his resurrected body. God's Spirit was alive in these groups as in Christ's own body. In these fragile communities Jesus and his deepest hopes survived.

The charm of this metaphor of the body is its immediacy—its visceral and even sexual overtones. What do we know more intimately than our own bodies—even if this knowledge is a mixture of delight and distress? But Christians have long been hesitant about their bodies. Influenced by a cultural animosity toward the body that was especially virulent in the third and fourth centuries, our ancestors turned gradually away from the immediacy and fleshiness of this metaphor. The church became pictured as "the mystical body of Christ"—with the mystical overshadowing the body. Further, the church came to picture itself as the glorious body of Christ, the sinless gift of God. This enthusiastic picture tended to neglect the real wounds and deep scars that are a part of this graced body. Since Vatican II we have begun to return to a less mystical and more realistic appreciation of ourselves as the body of Christ.

Portraying a group of people—a parish or ministry team or social justice network—as a body has both sociological and religious advantage. The metaphor of a body highlights the complexity of a social system: different members with diverse needs contend toward harmony and effective action. The group is more than an amalgam of its distinct members; it is more than the sum of its parts. Like a physical body, a diocese or religious congregation has a double ambition—coordination and graceful performance. The internal goal of coordination—our various parts working more in harmony than conflict—contributes to the external goal of effective action. The dancer or athlete (like the parish council or religious task force) strives to develop an inner coordination that issues in a graceful performance—one accomplished with competence, ease and delight. The secret ingredient in such a graceful performance is discipline: both the dancer and the community endure years of ascetical training to reach this gracefulness. The deception is that the final result looks so easy! But behind the virtuosity lie the virtues—the strenuous, repeated efforts of coordination and execution.

The Scriptures authorize us to picture the Christian community as a body: a complex social system needing coordination if it is to perform gracefully. Leadership may then be imaged as these exercises of coordination: the internal ordering of the body's various strengths for purposes of graceful and effective action. It is a process in which the entire body participates, even as the designated leaders play a special role.

This process of "ordering" has traditionally described the exercise of Christian leadership. The sacrament of "Holy Orders" celebrates the initiation of a new community leader. We "ordain" our leaders for service to the community. When we speak of leadership as a process of "ordering the body" we have yet to specify how the ordering takes place. How does leadership contribute to a social body's coordination and graceful performance?

In a hierarchical vision of the body, we tend to picture leadership as the head "giving orders" to the rest of the body. The head, where the regal power of reason resides, is placed above the other, inferior members. Such, of course, is the classical portrait of the human person as a "rational animal": reason controls and orders the body's passions, those unruly powers of sexuality, anger and imagination that so easily lead us astray. This dualistic vision of the human body was dominant in the cultures where Christianity first flourished; quite naturally, then, the body of the church was interpreted in this fashion. In a religious hierarchy, a male leader assumed the position of the head, giving orders to the lay and feminine members of the body.

A very different view of the body and its good order has begun to emerge, both in the American culture and in Christian experience. We have begun to envision the body (physical and social) not as a regal reason ordering the proletarian passions but as a consortium of powers. The physical body and the body Christian are both comprised of a mutuality of powers: affection, assertion and imagination complement and challenge reason in the complex process of ordering the body. Reason does not simply "order" or control the other vital powers of a human person. If reason plays a special role in coordinating these powers, it does so not as an independent authority but as a partner in the process of human maturing.

In this portrait of embodiment the task of ordering is a mutual and corporate one. Each power contributes to the good order and coordination of the whole. No power is merely passive, nor is any member inferior to the others. All the powers are needed for the building up of the body. Imbalance and a failure of coordination result when any one of these powers tyrannizes the others: if reason is exercised to the neglect of imagination and affection, a bright but unbalanced person is produced; when affections go unordered by assertion and reflection, our mood swings frustrate our commitments and threaten our fidelity.

This vision of the body allows for both mutuality and spontaneity. Reason is not exiled above the body nor constrained to play a detached, superior role. Affection is not restricted to the play of hormones; imagination is not dismissed as an irresponsible flight of fancy. The community of the body (our physical body and our religious tradition) is neither a monarchy nor a patriarchy. It is a more interdependent arena of differing powers, each with a specific gift to contribute to the whole.

The "ordering" task of leadership is to coordinate the body's various powers in graceful and effective self-expression. But in this view of the embodied person the power to order is one among several that are necessary for its life. While reason contributes its order and coordination, its tendencies toward control and abstraction must be tamed by the affections and seasoned by the imagination. In intimacy with imagination and affection, the power of reason is matured and made more human. In intimate league with the other mature adults in a faith community, leaders become both more human and more powerful.

We began this section with the suggestion that we picture leadership as the *internal process* by which a body orders itself. Yet even within this metaphor of the body Christians have pictured leadership in an external and dualistic fashion: the superior head gives orders to an unruly body; a hierarchical reason "husbands" its feminine body; clerical leaders seek to direct the body's lay members. We have outlined here a more wholistic vision that is emerging within the church: plural powers within the body struggle together toward a unified and coordinated expression. In this interpretation, reason and headship are invited to a greater intimacy and mutuality with the other powers, while still playing a special role. In the body Christian, ministerial leaders are likewise coaxed toward a greater intimacy with other members of the body, while retaining a crucial role in the process of ordering the body of Christ. The New Testament image of the Christian community as the body of Christ lures leaders back from their heady exile into the body of the community and calls all its members to participate in the building up of this body.

FOUR APPROACHES TO LEADERSHIP

This theology of the body, with its implications for leadership, is paralleled in recent developments in the social sciences. Sociologists and psychologists have long been fascinated by the phenomenon of leadership. The history of this continuing interest is marked by several significant shifts. Early research looked at leadership as a *personal quality* that belonged to the leader. The next wave of studies concentrated on the context in which leadership is exercised, introducing the terms *situational leadership* and *functional leadership* into the discussion. The current emphasis is on leadership as a *system,* part of the complex process of a group's life. Each of these orientations shows us something important about leadership. Learning from these different approaches, we can better appreciate both the power and the limits of the leader's role.

The Personal Traits of the Leader

Initial attempts to understand the dynamic of leadership focused on the personality of the leader. Aware that some people perform better than others in leadership roles, researchers set out to explain this difference in terms of personality. Leadership was approached as an individual characteristic or "trait," an ability that some people have and others do not. Leadership ability was assumed to be a relatively stable quality, available to the leader in whatever setting he finds himself (and the pronoun is appropriate here, since this approach tended to see leadership as a properly "masculine" trait). Since it was understood to be a personality factor, leadership ability was expected to be consistently available: a person with the trait should be able to lead in all—or at least most—situations and persons without the trait would be expected to function as followers.

This approach to leadership tended to emphasize our "heroic" expectations of our leaders: they should be exceptional individuals, gifted by a mysterious ability to prevail in difficult situations. By studying those who were particularly effective in leadership positions (and usually choosing the most heroic examples—Napoleon, George Washington, General MacArthur) researchers hoped to identify the personality factors involved. Once these elements of the leadership trait were identified, it was thought, the information could be used to determine in advance the "leadership potential" of people being considered for important positions.

This approach fell into disuse after several decades of research failed to produce any clear results. Real leaders could be identified and their traits could be described. But rather than pointing to a single quality that was common to all these people, the research findings revealed a remarkable array of personality factors. From situation to situation, the characteristics of those who functioned as "good leaders" were different. Studies in different group settings came up with contradictory findings: some effective leaders were "take-charge" types who gave clear directions and closely followed their subordinates' progress. In other situations the effective leader had a low-key style that left much to the initiative of other people. Among successful leaders were found both the gregarious and the shy, both conciliators and challengers, both "idea"-persons and "people"-persons. In the face of mounting evidence, it became clear that these differences were too diverse for leadership to be adequately understood as a single personality trait.

The search for a distinct "leadership trait" proved to be futile, but something important was learned along the way. Most of us know from our own experience that the personal qualities of those in leadership roles *are* important. Research findings reinforce this "common-sense" conviction but add important nuances. The personality of a leader frequently has a "make-or-break" influence on a group. A leader's consistent inability to accept criticism, for example, usually inhibits a group's efforts to pursue its goals. A group whose leader has become comfortable with conflict and debate will probably be livelier and more effective in its deliberations.

FOUR APPROACHES TO LEADERSHIP

Leadership is a Personality TRAIT

   Insight: Effective leaders have personal qualities that contribute to their success in the role.

Leadership is a Relationship between LEADER AND FOLLOWER

   Insight: Effective leaders respond to the maturity of their followers.

Leadership is a Relationship between LEADER AND GROUP

   Insight: Effective leaders insure that groups deal with both internal (belonging) and external (performance) tasks.

Leadership is a PROCESS OF GROUP INTERACTION

   Insight: Effective leaders nurture the larger network of relationships through which groups act effectively.

But in different settings quite different personality factors become significant. Social science research began to recognize the special influence of the *setting* on the leader's effectiveness. Personal qualities, then, have something important to do with leadership, but there is much more involved than individual ability. With this realization, research shifted from an exclusive focus on the leader to include an awareness of the leadership setting.

The Relationship Between Leader and Followers

This new approach broadened the study of leadership by looking at the group as well as its formal "head." The insight here recognizes that the group's effectiveness does not depend on the leader alone. The leader's success is significantly influenced by the group. Guided by this conviction, researchers set out to study "situational leadership" or the influence of the group on the leader's behavior.

By widening the focus of study, "situational leadership" reminds us that the leader does not operate in isolation. In concept, an examination of the leadership "situation" could consider many things—the group's task, its history, its environment, and more. In practice, however, the focus of research was often psychological. Leadership began to be interpreted as a relationship between leader and follower. The "situation" came to be understood, for the most part, as the maturity level of group members. Leaders were advised to be alert to the differences that exist among group members and to use this awareness to guide their behavior. Where people are experienced and competent, leaders were encouraged to reward initiative, accept dissent, encourage members to become involved in the processes of decision-making. Where group members are less confident or less trained for the task, more directive behavior on the part of the leader was recommended—setting out clear procedures, supervising the work closely, reinforcing order and control.

Take an example in ministry. A priest serving for some years in an ethnic parish becomes an effective leader in this community. His style is somewhat parental: strong and caring, he is definitely the person "in charge." The parishioners depend on him in many ways; they look to him for guidance in their personal lives and defer to his judgment in parish matters. They also display a fond affection for the pastor, appreciative of his dominant style of leadership. This priest is then transferred, assigned as principal in a large suburban Catholic high school. Suddenly his community has radically changed. Here the teachers and administrators expect to be his colleagues in ministry, not his children. They demand collaboration rather than instruction. A style of leadership that had been effective in one setting is suddenly outmoded. A new relationship between the leader and the other members of the community is demanded; new skills and virtues will be necessary for the priest's leadership to be effective in this changed setting.

A major contribution of the "situational" approach, with its psychological emphasis, is the recognition that leadership is a relationship. But this is usually understood to be a *one-to-one* relationship. To be effective, the leader is advised to establish an appropriate relationship with each subordinate, a relationship that responds to the particular strengths and needs of the follower. This is good advice, to be sure, as far as it goes. But such an understanding of leadership is not without its pitfalls. A major problem is the image it suggests. In most discussions of situational leadership the leader stands, as it were, at the hub of a wheel. The relationships that are assumed to be most important are those that go out from the designated leader, like spokes from the hub. We are easily left with the impression that leadership is *exclusively* the set of relationships established by the person in charge.

As this happens, we start to slip back into seeing the leader as the "source" of the group's effectiveness. The contributions of other people become invisible. Relationships among group members are downplayed: if the person in charge isn't involved, what can such relationships have to do with leadership?

The Relationship Between the Group and the Leader

Leadership happens between leader and follower: this advances our understanding but still does not tell the whole story. Researchers became increasingly aware that leadership involves more than a series of one-to-one relationships; the leader's task is not consumed in directing *this* person, *that* person, and all the other individuals in the group. Leadership "goes on" as part of a group's life. The leader, therefore, must be involved with the life of the group as a whole, not just with individual members.

To be effective, a leader has to understand how a group actually functions. Guided by this conviction, social scientists began to look closely at what goes on in groups—and the discipline of group dynamics was born. The discussion of "functional leadership" is rooted in an appreciation of the necessary dynamics of group life. If a group is to survive and flourish, attention must be paid to both its internal life (what goes on among the members) and its broader purpose (the reason the group exists—its goal or task or "product"). If either of these is overlooked, the vitality of the group is likely to be threatened.

In a group, for example, in which members are distracted by conflict among themselves or preoccupied by concern about where they fit in the status hierarchy, it is likely that the accomplishment of the common task will suffer. On the other hand, a group that focuses exclusively on "getting the job done," with little concern for the relationships that develop among members, risks losing the commitment of its people. As participation becomes defined more and more in terms of productivity, the emotional satisfactions of belonging to the group are diminished. This often leads to a loss of enthusiasm among members, which gradually erodes their commitment to the common task as well.

Observers of religious communities have become more aware of the importance of this dual focus in a group's life. One type of leader may so emphasize the interpersonal life of a community that all its energies are consumed in its care for and celebration of its own life; the group has little energy left with which to reach out to serve others and to contribute to the demands of social justice. In another group, a leader urges the members to focus all their attention on the important tasks of their ministry. Little time is given to relaxing, being together, sharing their faith. Gradually the community's members lose their enthusiasm for living together and community life stagnates.

For a group to remain alive, then, relationships must be maintained and tasks must be accomplished. The wise leader makes sure that the group pays attention to both. This does not mean that *only* the leader has a contribution to make here; nor does it mean that the leader has to be formally "in charge" of everything that touches on the group's morale and productivity. It is seldom that any one person, whether designated as leader or not, has the talent or time to respond to this range of responsibilities. More importantly, keeping relationships alive and doing the job well are responsibilities of the *group,* not of the leader alone.

The insight of the group dynamics approach, then, is that the leader should be aware of the needs of the group's internal life as well as the demands of the job. With such an awareness, the effective leader acts to insure that the group pays attention to both these dimensions. Sometimes the leader will take direct action—planning a party to upgrade morale in the office, intervening in a conflict between subordinates, replacing a staff member whose performance has consistently been poor. But more often leaders contribute to group functioning indirectly—by establishing a climate of trust, supporting effective procedures, facilitating the work of others.

But the functional approach to leadership, too, has its limits. If it emphasizes that the leader acts in relation to the group as a whole more than to individuals, it still encourages us to picture the leader as somehow beyond the group. The leader here is likely to be imaged as standing "outside," helping the group deal with its tasks. "The leader" and "the group" can still seem to exist as two separate, even autonomous, realities.

But the leader and the group are not separate realities. We are coming to see that the designated leader, the formal head of the group, is *part* of the larger network of effective group behavior. Leadership is a dynamic *of* that network and does not exist apart from it. Leadership is to be studied, and judged, in terms of the effectiveness of the relationships that characterize the group as a whole.

Leadership: A Process of Group Interaction

In the social sciences today, leadership is being defined as the system of relationships through which a group acts effectively. Each of the previous approaches highlights a partial truth: the effectiveness of leaders is influenced by personality factors, by responsiveness to different levels of maturity among group members, and by an ability to foster a vital balance in the dynamics of the group's life. But each of these orientations attempts to understand leadership primarily in terms of individual behavior. Concentration on the activities of one of the members of the group—the person designated as "leader"—has distracted attention from what is going on in the group as a whole. This shared preoccupation has led earlier researchers to neglect the most fundamental factor of leadership, its reality as a process.

Leadership is not just the influence that one person (or even a small group of persons) has on the rest of us. Leadership is much more adequately seen as a *process of interaction*. This process includes everything that goes on in the group that contributes to its effectiveness. Leadership exists when group members deal with one another in ways that meet their needs and contribute to their goals. Understood in this way, leadership includes all those elements in a group's life that *lead to* its survival and growth.

This approach is rooted in the understanding of the group as a system. A system is a network of interlocking parts. In a system each part is connected to the whole. The network is interdependent, so that a change in any component part has impact on the system as a whole.

Every group, every community, every organization is such a system. Understood as a system, a group is composed of interdependent relationships. When there is a change in one relationship, all the other relationships are affected; the whole group is involved. Here the social science view reinforces a theology of the body: a group is a social body whose parts must interact harmoniously for its inner coordination and external effectiveness.

Leadership thus becomes recognized as an intimate aspect of this interlocking system. It is not just what one person in the group "has"; nor is it what the leader alone does. Leadership arises in the interaction of the body's members. Leadership "happens" in the give-and-take of relationships that develop in the group, relationships among members as well as those involving the officially designated leaders. Properly speaking, then, leadership "belongs" more to the group than to an individual placed in a formal role.

The insight of this systemic approach is that leadership is a process; it is what goes on throughout the group, *leading* a system or body toward effective self-expression. In a group that is very passive, an individual leader may well provide most of the initiation and influence that make up the group's life. But in most communities a wide range of initiation and influence is at play. Leaders respond to these actions—encouraging, resisting, coordinating—as well as contributing their own ideas and energy to the process. Leadership, in this interpretation, includes not just the formal leader's actions and reactions but all those relationships that *lead to* the group's development. Leadership *is* that complex interplay of forces in a vital community's ongoing life.

This does not mean that groups no longer need formal leaders. Those persons designated to be "in charge" have an indispensable role. The systemic insight helps to clarify more precisely what this role is. Designated leaders are not to *supply* the group's effectiveness; their role is to *nurture* the group's effectiveness, fostering the network of relationships through which the group cares for itself and pursues its goals.

Leadership, we are suggesting, is an ongoing transaction. It is "what goes on" among people in the group, helping them to act together in ways that are satisfying and effective. Leadership behavior, then, covers a wide range of activities, sometimes initiated by official leaders but very often—especially in groups that are functioning well—undertaken by other members also. Leadership activities include all those interactions that energize group life—reinforcing the sense of personal commitment among the members, forging individual needs and values into collective purpose, mobilizing the group's resources to face the demands of change.

This orientation invites leadership back into the community. It encourages us to reflect on our leaders as part of the group's life. Neither independently empowered nor heroically gifted, religious leaders participate in and serve the community's response to God's power among us.

THE TASKS OF THE LEADER

The leader's role, as we have seen, is to help the group act effectively. How is this to be done? In different groups, even at different stages in the life of the "same" group, the challenge will be different. A group just starting out (a newly hired staff of a diocesan office for ministry training, for instance) may need a directive person in charge, someone who is an expert at the task and can show the others how to proceed. But as the staff matures the leader will expectably become less dominant, more a coordinator than an initiator. A group assembled to make policy (a parish council, for example) often thrives with a leader who plays a mediating role, who can welcome differing opinions and encourage workable compromise. The head of a large organization—a hospital or social welfare agency—will have administrative responsibilities that are not part of leadership in a small informal setting, such as a support group among married couples.

The precise job description of the leader, then, will differ from group to group. But, as the work of Warren Bennis, Rosabeth Kanter, William Lassey and other students of organizational life have shown, there are some common expectations. Whatever the group's stage or setting, effective leaders must be able to *nurture commitment* and *foster collaboration.*

Leaders Nurture Commitment

Commitment is always about meaning; a sense of commitment thrives when people share a vision that calls out their allegiance. This common vision is a source of a group's energy. The shared vision for a group of Christians includes the values of the gospel and the ambition for the Kingdom of God. The effective leader helps group members to stay in touch with these deepest beliefs and, from these shared convictions, to draw the strength they need for effective action.

For most Christians the Sunday liturgy is a major occasion for revisiting their best religious hopes. In preaching, leaders call the community to rekindle their vision. The official leader of a group need not be an excellent preacher; but the leader must *see to it* that good liturgy and effective preaching thrive in the community.

To nurture commitment, leaders must be able to encourage the conversation about values. This can be done formally, when a pastoral team assists the parish council in drafting a statement of the beliefs and hopes they hold in common. But these formal efforts may well fail if the atmosphere in the group does not support the dialogue about our deepest values. For our mission statements to be more than simply rhetorical, they must be rooted in our experience. Practically this means that our confessed, public values must be intimately linked with our best hopes and deepest needs.

For most of us, our needs and hopes are kept very private. Often we are not even sure what it is we desire most deeply or what we most genuinely need. We may feel uncertain how our own unspoken hopes mesh with the message of Jesus Christ. We can feel particularly vulnerable in a discussion about our values, since these touch so significant a part of ourselves. Before the formal conversation about shared vision can take place, the group must develop a level of trust and self-disclosure that permits the probing for deeper values. Leaders cannot demand such trust; they must be able to model the kind of self-exploration and honesty that encourages others to share their best and deepest hopes.

Leaders can also nurture commitment by strengthening the ways that group members are linked as an effective "we." This "we" depends on the development of a group identity, a shared awareness of what it is that holds us together. Group identity happens around what we believe together. The source of identity can be internal to the group (our shared goals and values) or external (a perceived threat or a common enemy). In either case the awareness that "we are in this together" reinforces the conviction that "we need one another." It is often the leader who keeps before the group the facts of its interdependence. Sometimes by celebrating the group's successes, sometimes by recalling the dangers still to be faced, leaders remind us that the "we" is important. "We can do more together than any one of us alone." Where such a realization is alive, commitment to the group is high. Group commitment can be nourished in a number of ways. In ordinary times a parish festival or commemorative liturgy celebrates our unity; in extraordinary times—a disaster or crisis—leaders can assist a group to grieve, examine itself and rebuild.

In many parishes today there are ongoing small groups in which adults come together to share their faith, honestly and concretely. These groups help rescue a large parish from a general feeling of anonymity. Here the vision of the gospel is rekindled and social cohesion is pursued. These groups can be effective, as well, in bringing faith to expression in ministry. As we share our best hopes for our Christian life we come to see how those hopes must find concrete expression. Leaders—both those within the groups and those with broader parish responsibility—often play a critical role in helping members to avoid the subtle temptations of self-absorption and elitism that sometimes accompany the small group experience. Helping these groups remain in touch with the community's shared vocation, leaders assist the effort to bring faith to expression in service.

As with preaching, every leader need not be skilled in the formation and guidance of small groups. But leaders are called to *see to it* that such deep and continuing conversations about faith and mission occur.

Leaders Foster Collaboration

The goal of leadership, as we have seen, is to strengthen the group's effectiveness. A leader must be able to help the group move its commitment into collaborative action. The hope that we share as Christians—of a world transformed by justice and love— must energize us to act together effectively in pursuit of this vision. The leader fosters such collaboration by supporting efforts (1) to mobilize the goup's collective resources and (2) to devise workable strategies for joint action.

Mobilizing the group's resources includes both *generating* and *focusing* its strengths. The goal is to make "more" of the group's power. Effective leaders take steps to help the group grow in both competence and confidence.

A group's resources are mobilized in part by helping people get better at doing what needs to be done. Programs of communication skills for parishioners involved in ministry with families in crisis; a study group scheduled for discussion of a recent pastoral letter from the American bishops; a training sequence for religious educators and youth ministers; support workshops for members of the parish task force on housing for the elderly—these efforts enhance a group's power to act effectively. Here again, the leader's task is seldom to provide the training personally. But effective leaders *see to it* that this kind of skill development is made available; they take the practical steps necessary (realistic scheduling, manageable fees, convenient transportation, baby-sitting provided) to enable group members to participate.

But sometimes it is not the acquisition of new skills that is required but the recruitment of talent and experience that already exist. Effective leaders create an atmosphere that invites people to recognize their gifts and to offer them to the tasks of the Kingdom. This can involve supporting parishioners in their responses to the ethical challenges they face in their occupations. There are organizational actions that can be taken as well. Leaders can work to bring more of the group's expertise into play by broadening the structures of evaluation and accountability: calling together a committee of teenagers to recommend programs for young people, for example, or establishing a parish school board to share responsibility for educational policy and financial planning. Through working committees and advisory panels, through the short-term task force and standing commissions, steps can be taken to include more of the group in the ongoing processes of decision-making.

Structures of collaboration are critical to a group's effectiveness, but these organizational efforts are seldom sufficient on their own. For collaboration to flourish there must be a sense among the members that *this* group is worthy of my strengths and respectful of my needs. The leader is often critical in creating and safeguarding this atmosphere in a group—building up the images and myths through which the members celebrate the significance of the group, supporting a climate of trust and acceptance among members. The leader is not the only person who nurtures this deeper appreciation of the group's worth. The talents for storytelling and celebration required here are likely to be spread throughout the group. Here again, the leader's role is to *see to it* that this atmosphere of respect is sustained and that remedies are undertaken if mutual trust begins to erode.

Collaboration also requires strategies for joint action. Devising workable strategies involves the leader (and others in the group) in efforts to work out the best ways to focus the group's energies on shared tasks and common goals. There are important practical techniques that can help here—strategies of systematic analysis, problem-solving and planning that make up the tools of the discipline of organizational development. Our social justice committee's enthusiasm for providing support for families who are faced with unemployment will not of itself guarantee an effective program. A strategy of problem-solving and goal-setting can give more practical shape to these religious hopes.

Political awareness is as important as systematic analysis, since in every setting—both within the group itself and in the system that the group wants to influence—there are the formal structures of power and the informal structures of politics that must be dealt with. Before lobbying for subsidized housing for the elderly to be located in our parish we do well to learn about the political forces that have, until now, prevented such efforts. These efforts to devise workable strategies are a crucial part of religious leadership: they rescue virtue from rhetoric; they provide a practical and accountable means for putting our faith to work in the world.

This larger, systemic understanding of leadership does not resolve the complicated issues of leadership that confront the community of faith today, but it does help us state more precisely what the real issues are. Discussions of religious leadership have often focused on the individual who is the formal leader (priest or pastor) to the detriment of the community's other resources. The return of leadership from exile to its true home in the Christian community is the invitation of the Spirit today.

REFLECTIVE EXERCISE

We invite you to test this notion of leadership as a part of a group's life against your own experience. We suggest the following exercise.

From your many social involvements, select a group or community that you know well and that is important to you. Bring to mind, for a moment, the people involved in that group and its recent history.

Recall a recent experience of this group acting at its best—functioning well as it pursued a project or faced a crisis or accomplished a goal.

List for yourself now the responses that went into the group's success—suggestions made, actions taken, conflicts resolved.

In the interplay of these different responses, what was the formal leader's role? How did the formal leader contribute to the group's success? Were there ways in which the formal leader hindered the group's effectiveness?

What are your own learnings here about leadership as a group process?

ADDITIONAL RESOURCES

The history of the ministry of ordering and the theology of "Holy Orders" is a complicated one. Early on this ministry was understood as an entry into an elite "order" or class of leaders (clergy). Such a static and elitist approach disguised the service aspect of ministering to the good order of a faith community. For some of the historical details of the understanding of "orders" and ordination, see Nathan Mitchell's *Mission and Ministry* (Michael Glazier, 1982), pp. 209ff. The eminent biblical scholar Ernst Kaesemann explores Paul's special intent in developing the metaphor of the body of Christ in his article, "The Theological Problem Presented by the 'Motif of the Body of Christ,' " in *Perspectives on Paul* (SCM Press, 1971).

There is a rich literature in the social sciences dealing with leadership. Rosabeth Moss Kanter examines the workings of power and leadership in the corporate structure in *Men and Women of the Corporation* (Basic Books, 1976). Warren Bennis' contribution to organizational strategy spans several decades; his latest book, *Leaders* (Harper & Row, 1985), coauthored with Burt Nanus, identifies four sets of skills that characterize effective leaders. In *Leadership and Social Change* (University Associates, 1983) William R. Lassey and Marshall Sashkin assemble a "state of the art" collection of essays on leadership in a variety of organizational settings. Edgar

H. Schein explores the dynamics of the leader's role in *Organizational Culture and Leadership* (Jossey-Bass, 1985).

In *Leadership in a Successful Parish* (Harper & Row, 1986) Thomas Sweetser and Carol Wisniewski Holden offer a practical discussion of what is involved in the exercise of leadership in the parish setting. For effective strategies of problem-solving suited to the local community of faith, see J. Gordon Myers and John J. Lawyer, *A Guidebook for Problem Solving in Group Settings* (Sheed & Ward, 1985).

In *Leadership in Paul* (Michael Glazier, 1984), Helen Doohan examines Paul's developing understanding of the essentials of Christian leadership as expressed in his letters to local communities of faith. James C. Fenhagen treats issues of ministerial leadership in the systemic perspective in *Mutual Ministry: New Vitality for the Local Church* (Winston Press, 1977). Robert Greenleaf draws upon both biblical values and corporate examples in his discussion of *Servant Leadership* (Paulist Press, 1977). In *Liberating Leadership: Practical Styles for Pastoral Ministry* (Winston Press, 1986), Bernard Swain explores new models of pastoral leadership that have emerged in the church since Vatican II.

CHAPTER SIX

TOWARD A NEW VISION OF CHRISTIAN LEADERSHIP

"The king is dead; long live the king!" In this peculiar proclamation we admit that leaders perish and leadership survives. The death of a leader creates a traumatic gap in a community; the group's continuity and even survival are threatened. We act, in confidence or panic, to replace the leader. In this perilous transition we find not only a new leader; we sometimes find a new kind of leadership. Leadership—that function of group life so vital to its development—survives. But it sometimes survives in a very different form.

"The emperor has no clothes!" This is a delicate matter, a crisis of both intimacy and power. Who will break the news to the authorities? One meaning of this fable of the emperor's undress is that we invest our leaders with different robes and garments—different assumptions and expectations of leadership. The abstraction called "leadership" is a product of the community. We not only choose our leaders; we choose to portray them in certain ways—as parents, or shepherds, or princes. These metaphors are cloaks that both cover and define our leaders. Like any clothing, they become, in time, threadbare. They no longer decently describe our leaders. "The emperor has no clothes." We are compelled to outfit our leaders in new images and expectations.

In this book we are about the reimagining of leadership. As we seek to envision Christian leadership anew we need new lenses to assist our gaze. We need to aid our sight with certain convictions that are gaining increasing attention in Christian life today. In this chapter we will examine four such convictions. They concern our differences in strength, the virtue of dependence, the symbolic role of the leader and the distrust of dichotomies.

CELEBRATING OUR DIFFERENCES

Differences among us are "givens" in social life. Even if we are members of the same group we are not all the same. Some people characteristically initiate action while others usually respond. The opinions of some tend to carry more weight than those of others. We come to expect certain persons to take charge, accept responsibility, come up with the plan of action.

Some of these differences are artificial: for example, many of the advantages enjoyed by whites (at the expense of minorities) or by men (at the expense of women) are rooted in biases that are part of a larger cultural inheritance. But not all the differences in our social experience are artificial. We *are* different in many important ways. She has a clear analytical mind; I have considerable emotional stamina; he possesses a lively imagination. The critical issue is not whether we find real differences among us but what we make of them: in our life together, what significance do we give to our differences in strength?

In community life our abilities equip us in different ways—for planning or playing, comforting or confronting, suggesting new visions or managing details. Christians acknowledge these different strengths and talents as charisms. These particular gifts, so important in Paul's vision of community and ministry, are the ordinary and necessary resources that energize the church. Every group of believers is gifted by the Spirit with a variety of strengths. The vitality of the group is rooted in the very diversity of these gifts.

Some of the differences among us are personal, rooted in our particular talents and limits. Other differences that arise among us are structural, rooted in decisions about how the tasks of the group are regularly shared among the members. We set out in our group's bylaws, for example, the responsibilities of those elected to office. Then we select people to exercise these rights and duties. After the election we accept the "difference" in impact between these designated leaders and other members of the group. We make these decisions about structural differences in power (the leader being given greater influence than others) to put order into our regular dealings with one another. Our hope is that this order will help us act more effectively as a group.

A group's power is rooted both in the personal strengths of its members (charisms) and in the structures of its community life (roles and offices). The proper use of power does not deny that these differences exist among us; it influences the ways the differences among us are to be understood.

What difference do our differences make? This is, perhaps, the most challenging question of social life. What do the differences among us mean? Are they signs of personal privilege or do they serve the larger purposes of the group? Does our diversity divide us into "superior" and "inferior" or is it the basis of our effective collaboration? Our answers to these questions shape the leadership structures of the community.

A new vision of Christian leadership will depend on how we interpret our differences. The human community seems drawn to vertical metaphors to describe differences. In this interpretation our differences divide us into the "up-down" categories of social life: better/worse; stronger/weaker; superior/inferior. Differences in ability are translated into differences in excellence. We ask which of our different strengths is better: is thinking more valuable than feeling? We are concerned to rank and prioritize our differences: is assertion or nurturance to be preferred? Such a vertical world, the product of our own interpretation, reinforces the dichotomies that infect social life: male/female; white/black; clergy/lay. In this up-down image our differences can be used to justify the structures of social inequality.

A vertical portrait of social life is not the only one available to describe our differences in strength. There are other images to guide our response to the question, What difference do our differences make? Two images that stand in contrast to the vertical view are *interdependence* and *mutuality*. In interdependence, we count on our differences to overcome personal limitations. In mutuality, we count on our differences to release new resources in our midst.

The image of interdependence invites us to understand our differences differently. It encourages us to view our strengths as complementary, to recognize our abilities as interconnected. Our differences in strength can link us in effective social life. It is because we are not all the same that we *need* one another. I need your creativity; you need my patient attention to detail. It is because we have different strengths that our collaboration leads to such rich results. I bring to the task my energy and enthusiasm; you bring long experience, with its seasoned sense of the best timing for success. To survive, the community needs a wide range of such resources— abilities to celebrate, to organize, to heal, to plan, to confront, to forgive. It is because we have a variety of these resources among us that our group thrives.

The metaphor guiding us here is no longer a hierarchy of strong and weak but a network of plural strengths. Seen through the lens of pluralism, our differences do not just set us apart from one another; they reinforce the bonds among us. We need one another's resources to make up for the lack we find in our own. Our differences in strength link us together in effective relationships of complementary support.

The image of mutuality takes us further. Mutuality, as psychologist Erik Erikson reminds us, goes beyond the experience of complementarity, where your strength makes up for my need and my resources compensate for your lack. In mutuality, we count on each other for the release of our full power. Experiences in our families or in active parishes remind us of this truth: in the genuine interplay of strength and weakness we create more than simply the sum of our separate resources. New strengths are generated when we link our lives in these ways.

In a group where mutuality prevails, we can come to savor this augmenting of power. Working with these people for a while, I begin to sense that something is different. "These people bring out the best in me." Surrounded by their gifts and encouragement, I discover new and surprising resources within myself. More talent or vision or energy seems available to me here. And I am not the only one to experience this special synergy. *We* are at our best when we work together, and "our best" goes well beyond what we had originally thought. There is more here than the sum of the members taken separately—more of me and more of us. In experiences of this kind we begin to taste the mutuality of power. The biological paradigm for this *extra* of power is, of course, procreation. Together we do something that was beyond our private potential. And we come upon a similar experience in the midst of a eucharistic liturgy: as our different gifts and concerns come together, our group becomes more than it was. In this celebration it is made stronger, more confident and forgiving. Our interaction has released more power among us.

Images of mutuality enable us to interpret the real differences among us more gracefully. We are able to bring to the group both our resources (less anxious about how excellent they will be ranked) and our weaknesses (trusting that there is sufficient strength here to make up for these lacks). In such an atmosphere we can come together, in our differences, to generate more power than we had imagined possible. Christians describe this miraculous increase of power in the group as grace. In concert, our strengths are surprisingly magnified. This community of fragile Christians becomes, to its own amazement, a sign of God's presence in the world. It becomes a grace for others, a sacrament.

THE POWER OF DEPENDENCE

Theologian Annie Jaubert describes the structures of power and authority in the earliest Christian communities as a "mutual, but asymmetrical dependence" (p. 26). The different members of the faith community shared a common dependence on Jesus Christ and the gospel and a mutual reliance upon one another. But in the ongoing life of the group this dependence was not perfectly symmetrical: as members contributed their various gifts and strengths, different roles and ministries emerged. Members all depended on one another, but in different ways. In these first communities leadership was recognized as "the responsibility of all and the charge of some" (p. 25). Every adult member was responsible for the good order of the group, though some received a special charge: leaders were designated to see to a responsibility that all shared. In highlighting this interplay of gifts and responsibilities, Jaubert underscores the importance of dependence in the exercise of Christian leadership.

Social scientists concur. In his analysis of research findings on small groups, for example, sociologist Richard Emerson notes that

> Power is a property of the social relation; it is not an attribute of [a single person]. . . . Social relations commonly entail ties of mutual dependence between the parties (p. 32).

Organizational analysts James Brewer, Michael Ainsworth and George Wynne reinforce this view:

> . . . the exercise of power is a function of the interaction between people. This "economy of power" is a reflection of our interdependence and of our need for what others can do for us. Power does not exist for human beings unless it becomes active in a collective sense (p. 12).

A mutual dependence guides a group's efforts to manage its power —a power which goes beyond personal possession. A new vision of Christian leadership is rooted in this shared conviction about dependence and power.

As American Catholics, there have been both cultural and religious forces among us that fostered a heroic portrait of the leader. Many of us have come to imagine that a good leader must have a strong personality and be gifted with the self-sufficiency to stand alone. Taken to its extreme, this cultural ideal pictures the leader as a "lone ranger." Self-reliance replaces collaboration; autonomy is valued over the ability to cooperate. This caricature makes it difficult for us to appreciate interdependence as a necessary resource of leadership.

To many of us, "interdependence" suggests that I am not sufficient for myself, that I am dependent on resources beyond my own, that I *need* other people. Such dependence seems shameful. To look to other people for emotional support or practical assistance contradicts our prevailing norms of adult maturity. Our culture's commitment to independence and the frontier virtues of "making it on my own" and "being beholden to no one" can be seen most sharply in the tendency to consider dependence a feminine trait. To need support and assistance is to be "womanly"—hardly a preferred attribute within the masculinized American ideal of leadership. It is difficult, then, for many of us to see dependence as a strength, as a resource of adult maturity. Yet dependence is built into social interaction. The ability to rely on other people is crucial in both love and work. Sometimes the dependence is structural. Often at work, for example, my being able to achieve my goals *depends* in some way on you—your cooperation, your formal approval, your timetable or budget or plan. Even more complicated is the emotional dependence that is a part of adult relationships. I need you, not just to achieve my goals but to be included, to feel secure, to know that I am loved.

To help us appreciate dependence as a mature strength, it may be useful to give some examples. To develop the intimacy that nourishes the long-term relationships of marriage and close friendship, I must be able to trust myself with you, even my needs. For such a relationship to mature, I must be able to rely on you—to count on your love, to be confident of your care, to trust that you will make your strength available to me in ways that will not diminish me.

My ability to depend on you in this way says a good deal about you—how you have treated me in the past, how trustworthy you have proved yourself. But it says even more, perhaps, about *me*. To depend on you requires a capacity to open myself, trusting that I am strong enough to display my need and strong enough to survive if you cannot or do not respond.

Dependence, the ability to rely on other people, is a resource in work as well. Teamwork, genuine collaboration, delegating responsibility—all these require that I can rely on other people. If it is only my own strength that I can trust, it is unlikely I will risk collaborating with others closely enough for their efforts actually to affect me. If, as a leader, it is only my own judgment or talent or generosity upon which I feel I can rely, I am likely to retain direct control of as many elements of the job as possible. As a member in a staff or team I am likely to insist on distinct areas of responsibility and autonomous spheres of action, trying in this way to avoid having to depend on other people to "come through."

There are occasions, to be sure, when leadership calls for direct control and autonomous action. We need, at times, to confront others or make difficult decisions; we need to guide a project forcefully to its conclusion. To be effective leaders requires that we become competent—and confident—in these sometimes lonely exercises of personal initiative. But to be trapped in this independent stance, not because the situation calls for it but because I cannot face the challenge of relying on other people—this is to be limited as a leader.

An appreciation of mature dependence will support the effort to develop more adequate structures of leadership. Effective social life —whether in families, in work settings, in religious congregations or in political life—demands that we be able to depend on one another. This kind of "dependability" requires a sense of personal power. To be dependable, I must be able to trust my own strength. I must have sufficient confidence in my own resources that I can count on them: they will "be there" when I need them, when other people need them. This confidence is rooted in the adult strength of independence—the conviction that my own resources are adequate to the tasks that I face.

But more is required. Mature "depend-ability" means that I can rely on other people. Well before we are involved in roles of leadership, most of us learn that we can count on more than just ourselves. I come to realize that there are occasions—in love, in work, in faith—when I can share a power that goes beyond "just me." There are times when I cannot, when I choose not to "go it alone." These experiences invite us into a wider experience of power. We learn here to participate in a process that escapes our exclusive control. These experiences also prepare us for the interplay of successful leadership.

To experience the interplay of power is to know that I need other people. For many of us this is not easy to acknowledge. It means that I have to face my own limits. I have to recognize that there are areas of my life where my own strengths are not sufficient. Gradually I must come to accept my limits, even my weaknesses, without undue shame. Maturing in self-acceptance, I can learn to depend on others in ways that enlarge rather than diminish me.

This is the adult face of dependence: I can count on the resources of other people as well as my own. I do not possess alone all that brings meaning and joy and accomplishment to my life. There are strengths beyond my own that I need. To ask for, to accept, these resources does not demean me. Rather it opens me to an experience of power that is shared.

It is when I can experience shared power in this way that I become capable of real interdependence—the genuine interplay of both strengths and limitations in the movement toward common goals. It is to this complex virtue of interdependence that leaders in the community of faith are challenged today.

THE SYMBOLIC ROLE OF THE LEADER

Leadership, power and authority: each of these touches chords deep in the human psyche. We carry volatile memories of leaders, both good and bad; we harbor strong feelings about those forceful persons who used their power, sometimes to harm us, sometimes to heal. Our reactions to authorities surprise us until we recall these histories of care and frustration.

We quickly become aware of the symbolic function of leaders: they stand for much more than themselves as they trigger our finest and basest responses. A community's best hopes and values become focused on them. And our leaders remind us not only of high values but of ancient angers with parents and of humiliations that cannot be forgotten. The assassins of John Kennedy, Martin Luther King and Indira Gandhi were attacking much more than these leaders alone.

Religious leaders even serve the perplexing function of representing God to the community. This world of symbol and value, the locus of the Holy, we will refer to as the extra-rational. By this perhaps peculiar term we wish to point to the more than rational aspects of leadership. We refer to the wealth of feelings, visceral memories, anxieties and delights that are aroused in any reflection on leadership. These moods and energies are not well served by their conventional title of "irrational." When we so name these feelings and moods we treat them as less than human, beyond the pale of regal, humanizing reason. These very human and quite influential aspects of any consideration of leadership tend to be neglected, even intentionally disguised, in more antiseptic "rational" discussions.

Admitting the extra-rational to our discussion, we glimpse the full ambiguity of our hearts. We acknowledge the tendency to distance our leaders from ourselves, attributing to them magical powers and elegant titles, investing them with heavy cloaks of authority. We also recall the deep comfort of having someone else in charge, to make the decisions and take the blame in times of trouble. And we remember that the too strong leader can prevent us from growing up, parenting us long after we have ceased to be children. Sometimes the extra-rational refers to the dark forces in a group that a demonic leader can evoke; memories of Hitler remain as bitter testimony to this extra-rational aspect of leadership.

Frightened by this face of power and leadership, analysts tend to overcompensate by addressing only the rational side of leaders. Theologian Martin Hengel, in his study of *Christ and Power*, provides an example of this rationalizing tendency. Hengel describes Jesus' charismatic leadership style as though it were wholly rational:

> In using pictures and parables it was not his intention to conceal in an esoteric, apocalyptic manner but above all, by rational argument alone, to explain and clarify, that is, to reach an *understanding* with the hearer. [His emphasis; p. 21.]

Lest we miss this distinction, Hengel adds: "Jesus did not seek to seduce his hearers in an irrational manner." The only choice appears to be rational (the discourse of a philosopher) or irrational (the machinations of a madman). But Jesus, like any good leader, touched groups at many different levels: with both reasoning and exorcism, he challenged others to respond to their own best visions.

From our most ancient collective memories, religious leaders have claimed to represent the sacred: prophets spoke in God's name; shamans conjured up spirits; priests offered sacrifices to appease God's wrath. Despite this heritage, many religious leaders are understandably uncomfortable in such a role. The Protestant Reformation, in its denunciation of any religious leader who dared to trade God's forgiveness for the appropriate donation, reinforced this hesitancy. The reformers' rejection of an official and elite priesthood changed the status of the ministerial leader, defrocking him of some of his symbolic, sacred potency.

Today both Catholics and Protestants are keenly aware of the highly ambiguous nature of the leader's role in representing God. We no longer see the priest as the sole representative of God in the community, or as the uniquely privileged mediator of the Holy to a group. But we disagree with those who judge this role to be simply the result of projection. In special moments of healing and preaching, of crisis and prayer, the religious leader does often stand in the place of our invisible God. And people do confer on leaders expectations and hopes, feelings of gratitude and blame that do not belong to the leaders as individuals. This is a necessary, if perilous, means by which an intangible God comes into touch with us.

An analogy of this peculiar but normal interaction of the leader and community may be found in the interaction of psychiatrists with their patients. The patient, *as a normal part* of the process of healing, often confuses the therapist with an earlier object of a frustrated affection or denied anger. This is a distortion (the therapist, in historical fact, is not the genuine object of the patient's love or rage) but it has a role in the healing process. The confusion is, for many, the *necessary route* from repression and illness to insight and health. In this transference the patient can come face to face with the troubling emotion; having brought this distress to the surface, the person can then begin to uncover its real origins.

By their profession, religious leaders announce God's presence, proclaim God's challenge, offer God's forgiveness. These activities elicit and evoke strong reactions. Religious leaders often find themselves too loftily praised or too heatedly attacked, as others attribute to them gratitude or blame that is really directed to God. The leader is tempted to intervene: "I didn't really do anything," or "I'm not the one to blame."

The titles that a community uses for its leaders often reinforce this kind of transference. When we call our leader "father," for example, we evoke both happy and painful memories of our own childhood. This title is meant to link the leader's care with that we received from our parent, as well as with God's creative affection. Referring to our leader as "reverend" is intended to remind us of our ambition to revere God: the use of this term encourages us to link our esteem for God to the respect we show the leader. In a period of profound religious change, we need to clarify the dynamics of these complex extra-rational processes.

Leaders can fail their symbolic role by turning in either of two directions. They may be tempted to refuse this bewildering aspect of their role: keenly aware of their unworthiness, they may opt instead for a more rational "manager's" role in the religious group, becoming the anomaly of a secularized religious leader. Others may be drawn to take themselves too seriously as God's stand-ins. Neglecting the humility required in this ambiguous role, they become defensive of their sacred status and insist on special rank and privilege in the community.

The movement of contemporary communities of faith to reimagine leadership confronts a special challenge here. We continue to remove from our leaders signs of their special religious significance: the distinctive clerical clothes of the priest and the special habits of women religious are replaced by ordinary clothing; honorific titles such as "reverend" are used less. By thus desacralizing our leaders, we are revising our estimation of how God acts through us and among us. The community recognizes that the religious leader often plays a special role in the encounter with God. But the leader does not do so *uniquely* or *exclusively*. The leader's role as symbolic representative of God is meant to remind us that every maturing Christian can and must assume this responsibility. At different times, each of us is called to challenge or comfort or forgive others in the community. As Christians we act in God's name—if we are bold enough to admit it. When we console a sick child or stand in patient presence with a despondent adult, they may taste in our assurance the solicitude of God. This is one of the ways that God's care becomes incarnated. In our everyday witness to our faith, we give God a place to be seen; in the special crises of our lives, our fidelity and hope bring others in touch with God.

The religious leader is someone who by profession stands, regularly, in the place of God. But leaders, by representing God (and inheriting the accompanying aura of both honor and abuse), do not relieve us of our part in this witness of faith. As religious leaders are treated as less sacred, we find they are more like us than we had suspected: they are sometimes weak, often given to doubts, limited by innumerable shortcomings—just like the rest of us. This experience of empathy closes the gap between the leader and the community; this may be why social analyst Elizabeth Janeway has described empathy as a "revolutionary emotion." By overcoming the distance between leader and group, empathy allows us to realize that "the powerful" are *like me*. This insight helps dispel the aura of magic that often accumulates around the role of a religious leader. Such empathy does not abolish the leadership role or obliterate its necessary structures. It can even allow us to better appreciate the real dilemmas that surround this office and calling.

Our leaders are like us. This insight brings with it another realization: we are also more like our leaders than we had been led to believe. We are called to do something of what they do—stand for God, represent the Holy, give a place for God to be revealed. It is, of course, incongruous that we should be representing God. Historically we attempted to overcome the incongruity by cloaking our religious leaders in robes of honor and titles of prestige. In this way, we hoped to make them more worthy of the task. As we recognize that every Christian is called to this dangerous role, we divest our leaders of their unique status and invite them to rejoin the community. Less sacred and separate, our leaders still bear the challenge to represent the Holy while calling others in the community to share more energetically in this witness. The fruit of this strategy is that the community itself, not just its official leaders, comes to stand as a public sign of God's presence in the world.

DISTRUSTING DICHOTOMIES

The effort to reenvision the connections among leadership, power and authority is beset with many difficulties. New images of the leader and of the process of authorizing confront more conventional expectations of social life. Deeply engrained convictions yield only reluctantly to new visions of community and leadership. Two strategies to assist this transformation seem especially important. These are the disciplines of distrusting dichotomies and avoiding abstractions.

The cultural inheritance of Western Christianity includes a dichotomizing vision of the world. Western thought has been inclined to picture life as divided between good and evil, men and women, soul and body. This split vision of reality provided a neatness and control to our bewildering world. It gave us categories with which to manage the endless flow of our social existence. It also provided a simple strategy for resolving conflicts and uncertainty: things must be either good or evil, either masculine or feminine, either body or spirit. A quick and clear choice restrained the complexity that threatened us on every side.

In this dualistic world dichotomies flourished: the leader was clearly distinguished from followers; clergy were separated from the laity. The threat of power was managed by naming it either good or evil (and most often evil, it seemed). Authority came to be seen as rooted either in a universal law or in the autonomous individual; it seemed to be the property either of a dominant leader or of an individual's conscience. Either/or became our choice in this universe of dichotomies.

Christians began to envision the world as divided between the sacred and the profane. Certain places and times were especially holy, while the rest of the world remained secular—not especially blessed. We acknowledged a clear distinction between the sanctuary and the "ordinary" world, between the "sacred ministers" and ordinary or lay Christians.

The advantage of such a dichotomy was that it allowed us to locate, in a world that is always bewildering, persons and places that were assuredly holy. But this emphasis of the sacredness of the sanctuary led, inevitably, to the neglect of God's abiding presence in the more mundane. The holiness of the workplace and the home became diluted and even ignored. To designate some among us as sacred by profession tempted us to deny the genuine, if less public, holiness of the rest of us.

Today this distinction between sacred and profane appears as decidedly unchristian: it fractures a world whose potential holiness the Incarnation attempts to reveal. We are increasingly aware that God regularly escapes the confines of the sanctuary and is active among us in locations we previously imagined as profane. And it is especially from these "secular" environments—the workplace and the home—that new leaders are appearing among us. A less dichotomous vision of Christian life assists the return of leaders from exile: not so different from other Christians, our formal leaders are invited to a new intimacy with the community of faith.

The revolution of modern life offers both a threat to and a resolution of this world of dichotomy not yet expunged from most of our hearts. The threat is the acknowledgment of a profoundly plural world. Our exercises of power so often seem to proceed from both "good" and "bad" motives; often enough these actions have both positive and negative effect. Authority is discovered in many locations—Scripture, law, conscience, a community's evolving insights. Leadership becomes pictured not as a male prerogative, exercised independently of a community, but as a group process by which many different resources are coordinated for the community's good.

The resolution of this world of dichotomy follows on a reimagining of our corporate life. In the practical life of a community dichotomies meet and merge: good and evil overlap in our midst and in our own hearts. The facile distinction of "us" and "them"—which seemed to authorize an intolerance of outsiders—becomes less persuasive. A clear delineation between women as nurturing and men as assertive becomes muddied in the practical life of a community. In the interaction of a vital religious community we find the well-learned distinction of clergy and laity is less and less convincing. In the mutual dependence of many Christian communities the world of dichotomies is perishing. As this long-maintained vision of life dies, traditional definitions give way. Who is the best leader here? What are women and men "supposed" to do? How do we coordinate the plural authorities of the gospel, hierarchical leaders and conscience? Our automatic answers no longer serve; we must weigh evidence anew and make choices based on a broader range of factors.

In this more complex world, the strategy of either/or becomes defensive and regressive. It compels us into choices that are safe but not truthful. We need to distrust dichotomies—to refuse the choice between power as either good or evil, between obeying *either* an infallible pope *or* an infallible conscience. Such choices have a storybook charm but are untrue to the world as it is being revealed to us. The revitalizing of community life, with its diversity of strengths and various authorities, empowers us to refuse these ancient but ungraceful dichotomies.

A second strategy, necessary in this time of reimagining leadership, is to avoid abstractions. This is a special challenge in a discussion of those aspects of our shared life that we name leadership and authority.

The human invention of abstract nouns is itself an example of an endeavor that is neither simply good nor simply bad. It is helpful to employ the shorthand of a single term like "leadership" when talking about this diverse and complex process of human interaction. By the abstract word "leadership" we mean all those exercises of initiating and influencing that *lead to* the group's growth, but it is swifter to simply say "leadership." Though we signify by the abstract word "authority" that continual process of protecting our deepest values, it is much simpler to just say "authority." But this shorthand leads, inevitably, to deception.

By summarizing complex behaviors in a single term we suggest a uniformity and constancy that are untrue. An abstract noun, such as "leadership" or "authority," objectifies a process, assigning it a stability and permanence that are fictitious. In time we come to picture authority as a separate entity, rather than as a fragile human activity. In the process of abstracting, we select would-be essential and unchanging elements of leadership or authority as representative of these group actions. If we simplify reality when we abstract it in this way, we also remove these processes of leadership and authority from our participation. Leadership as an abstract concept is difficult to deal with; the abstract noun "authority" is hard to put one's hands on. These abstractions separate us from the processes themselves, suggesting they are the domain of "experts"—philosophers or priests or politicians. Abstraction leads, finally, to the exile of authority and leadership beyond the life and control of the community.

In *The Evolving Self,* psychologist Robert Kegan explores this necessary but dangerous tendency of abstraction. Even the fundamental process of existing, that lifelong movement expressed in the verb "be-ing," comes to be imagined as an abstract noun, "being." A human person comes to be pictured as a stable and even static entity (a *being)* instead of as an evolving person (a *be-ing).* Abstracting, we tend to remove the life and energy and movement from reality. Seeking to either clarify or protect an aspect of life, we end by perverting it.

Thomas O'Meara, in his historical study of the *Theology of Ministry,* illustrates this tendency to abstraction in church life: the function of serving is made into a social status; the fluid interaction of community ministries is hierarchized into different strata of excellence. O'Meara summarizes this historical tendency: "service has become authority" (p. 111).

"Authority" is an especially troublesome abstraction. As we will examine in Part II, the human process of authorizing certain cherished values builds and preserves our shared life. Communities, institutions and laws are forged and purified through a continuing process. This process is crystallized at certain points: various sacred books are gathered into a canon of Scripture; customary ways of dealing with property, marriage and crimes are collected into a law code; leaders are designated by official ceremonies and formal titles. But a human reluctance around change, with its constant reexaminations and purifications, tempts us to transform this process of authorizing into abstract "authorities"—people and laws which first represent the process and then come to replace it.

It is our intent in this volume to avoid abstractions as much as possible. We will, of course, often fail. Hoping not to exhaust the reader with tedious circumlocutions, we will refer to "leadership" and "authority." But our preference will be for "leading" and "authorizing," terms that more adequately reflect the complex and changing processes involved in building up the Christian community.

REFLECTIVE EXERCISE

Each of us has a different personal history of dependence. This history influences our attitudes toward leadership and our participation in community life. Take some time now to reflect on your own experience with dependence.

First, note your response as you read the chapter's discussion of adult dependence. Where did you find yourself in agreement? Where at odds? What feelings arose in the reading?

Then consider your life these days. Where is being dependent a negative experience for you? Be as concrete as you can. What is it about the experience that is troubling or unpleasant?

Where in your life these days do you enjoy the strengths of being dependent? Again, be concrete. In what ways are these experiences positive for you?

In those situations where you experience others depending on you, what is your response? How is this experience a delight? How is it a burden?

Finally, what convictions do you bring from your experience to the larger discussion about structures of interdependence in the life of the church?

ADDITIONAL RESOURCES

Theologian Annie Jaubert's remarks on a community's "mutual but asymmetrical dependence" appear in "Les Épîtres de Paul: le fait communautaire," in *Le Ministère et les ministères selon le Nouveau Testament,* edited by Jean Delorme (Éditions du Seuil, 1974), pp. 16–33. Bengt Holmberg, in *Paul and Power* (Fortress Press, 1978), attempts to follow Jaubert's insight about the mutual dependence of social power (pp. 70, 118, 199), but his reliance on Weberian notions of "power over" (pp. 10, 126) makes this project difficult.

Erik Erikson's characteristically succinct comments on mutuality are found in *Insight and Responsibility* (Norton, 1964). Richard Emerson's discussion of interdependence appears in his article "Power-Dependence Relations" in *American Sociological Review* (February 1962). James H. Brewer, J. Michael Ainsworth and George E. Wynne explore the interdependence of power in organizational settings in *Power Management* (Prentice-Hall, 1984).

There is a long tradition of studying the extra-rational, though usually under the categories of the irrational and the daimonic. Two recent classics are E. R. Dodd's *The Greeks and the Irrational* (University of California Press, 1951), which examines the furies, rages and demons that inspired and bedeviled the ancient Greeks, and Rollo May's *Love and Will* (Delta, 1969), a provocative exploration of the daimonic (or, ambiguously potent) energies of love and assertion.

For a discussion, in a positive light, of the necessary extra-rational elements of religious leadership, see Bruce Reed's *The Dynamics of Religion* (Darton, Longman & Todd, 1978). F. G. Bailey offers a provocative consideration of extra-rational factors in small groups in *The Tactical Uses of Passion* (Cornell University Press, 1983).

In *The Future of Difference* (Rutgers University Press, 1985), Hester Eisenstein and Alice Jardine bring together a provocative set of essays exploring the significance of "difference" in the feminist perspective. On the paradoxical role of transference in healing, see Janet Malcolm's *Psychoanalysis: The Impossible Profession,* (Vintage Books, 1981). Elizabeth Janeway's remarks about empathy as a "revolutionary emotion" can be found in *Powers of the Weak* (Knopf, 1981).

For Thomas O'Meara's discussion of the tensions in church ministry between doing and being, see his *Theology of Ministry* (Paulist Press, 1983), pp. 110f., and p. 189. Robert Kegan confronts the tendency to make an abstraction of the process of human development in *The Evolving Self: Problem and Process in Human Development* (Harvard University Press, 1982).

PART II

A CYCLE
OF
EMPOWERMENT

CHAPTER SEVEN

EMPOWERMENT: PERSONAL AND SOCIAL

Power, authority, leadership: these dynamics shape our social life. When we think of them as separate, abstract forces we send them into exile. In so doing, we deprive the community of these resources. Power and authority and leadership are then portrayed as belonging to special people who stand apart from and above the group.

The return from exile requires a healing of our social imagination. We need to recall that power and authority are inner dynamics of community life. Power is not an entity that some persons possess; it names the various interactions, creative and destructive, by which we link ourselves with one another. Authority is not an abstraction; it is the process by which we sanction the patterns of power among us. Communally, we authorize those values that define our life together. In this way we interpret and preserve power in our shared lives.

In the chapters of Part II that follow, we will explore the social and religious processes by which we acknowledge and purify power among us.

THE FACES OF POWER

The confusion about power in human affairs arises from its many faces. Each of us has experienced power in a variety of guises. Two of the most memorable faces among our negative experiences of power are external constraint and internal compulsion.

Few of us forget the face of constraint. Someone—often a person in a position of authority—wielded power over us, compelling us to act against our will. We felt coerced and injured by an external force. Much of social life, from politics to warfare, sports this destructive face of power, reminding us of ancient scars even while inflicting new wounds.

If the face of power as constraint is well known to us, it may still confuse us by donning a friendly mask. "Authorities" may use power to do a favor for us. Their power seems to benefit us. But, having been helped, we do not feel stronger or even grateful. We feel indebted. The deception deepens as we then feel guilty for not being grateful. What lies beneath this friendly mask of power? Often a pattern of paternalism. A strong person cares for us, but the care is given for purposes of constraint. We are not enlivened by such powerful action but feel bound by it. This deceptive pattern does not increase our power; it enslaves us to another's strength. Little wonder that "power" has a bad reputation among us!

We have experienced power as external constraint; most of us have faced it as inner compulsion as well. Here again, power wears a destructive guise, but now it is in our own house. I may feel driven to excess in eating or drinking, or obliged to "succeed" at whatever cost. A compelling need to be liked or to avoid showing any sign of anger; a consuming effort to prove myself, again and again, before a demanding internal jury—in these obsessions, an interior power has gone astray. Though no external agent is constraining me, I still experience the negative force of power. And though such a compulsion is felt as totally private, we can trace its links with society: social imperatives of popularity or competition have successfully shaped our behavior. And social "solutions," such as alcohol or drugs, are invitingly available.

Benevolent Powers

Happily, these are not our only experiences of power. We meet power in its positive face as well. After a painful argument with a dear friend I feel spent, angry and wounded. It seems that an unbridgeable gulf has opened up between us. I lack the strength, or even the will, to try to cross this gap; we are estranged. Then, unpredictably and not by my own doing, I am stirred to seek forgiveness and reconciliation. In the midst of a depletion of energy I experience an unexpected power. I find myself empowered to do something for which I had no strength. Christians acknowledge such an event as grace. This face of power appears as a gift and an empowerment. We are given the power to perform an act that, left to ourselves, we could not do.

A similar empowerment may happen in our careers. A friend in the parish, in her late forties, finds herself regularly exhausted and without energy. She realizes that her job has lost its appeal. The work in which she has been successful until recently now seems like a career pursued to please her parents. She wants to change careers but has no energy, no idea of where to turn. After some months in distress she is surprised by the dawning of a new direction. In this desert of her life, she feels stirred by new possibilities. A powerful sense of personal vocation begins to emerge. Where has this come from? she wonders. Whatever the source, she feels blessed and grateful. She feels empowered by new purpose and renewed energy.

These experiences have to do with receiving power. Power comes from beyond ourselves, to heal or challenge us. We feel empowered. At other times we are able, perhaps to our own amazement, to hand on this gift of power. We are able to empower others.

Last year a friend of ours who is a teacher met a young woman in a course that she was offering. Impressed by her student's potential, the professor told her so. The young woman was startled. She seemed flattered by the attention but was unable to believe her teacher. The young woman had little sense of her own abilities. Over that semester and the next, the professor continued to meet with her regularly; a friendship deepened. Gradually the young woman began to believe in herself a bit more. She began to think about a new job; she carried herself more assertively; she grew more comfortable with her own strengths. We could see power moving through the professor's hopes and confidence into the young woman's life. One person was empowering another. The older woman was generating more power, enhancing rather than "losing" her own power in the process.

This active empowerment is happening today in many small group settings. A priest is designated the head of a planning group in a parish. For six months the planning progresses smoothly with his strong leadership. The group enjoys assisting its leader in exploring important questions for the parish. But then the group's comfort is jarred; the priest suggests that the members begin to take on larger responsibility. This suggested shift in power is unsettling: how can they trust themselves as much as they trusted him? Yet he is resolute, offering practical recommendations to help the planning team draw more on its own resources. The priest here is letting go of power. As the group matures, he encourages them to acknowledge and trust their own power. But this letting go does not abandon the group to impotence. As he lets go, power passes into the group itself. Gradually the group experiences itself becoming more confident and effective. His letting go of power has empowered them.

EMPOWERMENT—THE PERSONAL CYCLE

Amid the many faces of power—the creative and destructive forces at play inside us and around us—we can discern patterns of power in our lives. Our adult careers and vocations depend on three distinct episodes of power.

The maturing of power in personal life is rooted, first, in a *recognition*. We must come to identify the gifts and abilities that give shape to an adult vocation. Without this recognition, however gradually achieved, we do not know who we are and what we are to do. This recognition has its special season in our early adult years as we move toward commitments of career and intimacy. But it endures for a lifetime as we continue to learn about ourselves and hear new invitations from God. This recognition of graceful power must be matched by a recognition of the destructive patterns of power in our life: the tendencies and temptations that regularly threaten our graceful participation in life. When these forces go unnamed and untamed, they defeat both our charisms and our conscience.

Recognition carries a nuance of receptivity: we are brought to see our gifts and a potential direction for our lives. We are graced with a recognition of our temptations and sinfulness. These gifts of recognition strengthen us for the mature exercise of power.

As these recognitions of power take shape, we are invited to choices and decisions. Enlightened about the potential of our gifts and our sinfulness, we must make adult commitments. In decisions about our relationships and careers, we give these recognitions a special authority. We take up the lifelong process of authoring our vocation. We choose paths to develop our potential; we make concerted efforts to curtail the influence of the destructive forces in our lives. In these efforts and assertions, we authorize *this* way of living a Christian life. We decisively join our abilities and energies to other lives: this partner, that parish, this religious congregation, these colleagues in a life's work. By such authoritative acts we give our hopes and values a place to live. In the earlier stage of power we recognized our gifts and charisms. In this second stage of personal authority our conscience is tested and matured. We choose, conscientiously, those jobs and partners with which to pursue our best hopes. In this season of power our conscience matures, through trial and error, into the inner authority that the Christian community needs.

As our adult lives unfold, we continue to meet these faces of power: the negative guises of constraint and compulsion; and the graceful faces of being empowered and being able to empower others. As we continue to mature, we are repeatedly invited to purify our relationships with power. I may find, in my late forties, that I have become too controlling in a community. Or a personal relationship has become destructive, or even died. Or a value pursued with vigor since my twenties has now become an idol: rigid, nonnegotiable, compulsive. In various ways, mild and dramatic, our lives demand attention and purification. Though we are blessed with charisms and guided by good consciences, we continue to fail our deepest values. We never outgrow the need for conversion. This third invitation, to purify parts of the life that we are authoring, usually entails a new recognition. I recognize a forgotten value or remember a dream that had been neglected. In purifying my life I begin the cycle again with a new or remembered recognition.

The maturing of my personal life moves through this cycle of empowerment: I recognize the power of God's gifts and charisms in my life; I then authorize my vocation, in choices of conscience and in my commitments of career and intimacy. And I continue to be challenged to purify the authoritative decisions of my life. Each step in this cycle is part of an empowerment: we repeatedly acknowledge, and choose, and purify patterns of power in our lives.

But this cycle does not just chart our individual journeys. Communities follow a similar cycle of empowerment. A diocese or school or ministry team moves through a comparable evolution. Even the Christian tradition itself matures along a similar path.

EMPOWERMENT—THE SOCIAL CYCLE

Recognizing, authorizing, purifying—these movements mark the ordinary, even predictable, stages in the development of a group's power. A community moves from recognizing its strength and needs, through a period of authorizing certain patterns of power in established structures, to a continual purifying of the distortions and rigidities that inevitably appear within its life.

Recognizing patterns of power is a special feature of the earliest stage of a group's life. As a parish begins, we look about to identify our resources and shared values. As we acknowledge our special strengths and needs, we ask: "Who are we?" This beginning stage is quickly followed by an effort of authorizing. We ask: "What should we become?" Our responses to this question initiate the authoring of our common life. We begin the long process of authorizing our style of Christian community. A third necessary movement of purification follows. As a community, we need to correct the overemphases and abuses which unavoidably accompany our efforts to build a common life.

Each stage of this continuing cycle contributes to the empowerment—the maturing of power—of a community. Originating but fragile insights are developed and safeguarded in authoritative structures which, in turn, require correction and purification. Power and authority do not reside exclusively in any one stage. The squandering of a community's power can occur at any point: we may fail to acknowledge our gifts or our special call. Or we can refuse to develop the structures that will safeguard our values. Or we neglect the ongoing conversion demanded of even the most conscientious community.

Recognizing Power

Religious traditions begin as charismatic leaders proclaim special patterns of power in the world. The life of Jesus Christ, as we shall examine in the next chapter, is the story of such charismatic leadership. Jesus recognized in an especially evocative way certain patterns of power that are inscribed in human life. He acknowledged and emphasized the elusive power to forgive. He celebrated the surprising ability to nourish one another in shared meals. He gave special attention to the power to confront the demons of compulsion and obsession that beset every society. Each of these is a complex set of social relationships. Each is a pattern of power that is easily forgotten or disguised.

Jesus' recognition of these forces imbedded in human affairs was not a private piety. He brought others to recognize these patterns of power as part of the Creator's care for us. This recognition was so compelling that a new religious movement was generated. The first communities of Christians struggled to preserve and safeguard the revelation of Jesus. His followers sanctioned certain written accounts of his life. They gradually developed customs and rules to keep them faithful to Jesus' values. These first Christians formalized rules for liturgical celebration and designated some in the community as their leaders. Jesus' witness to certain patterns of power was gradually embodied in a religious heritage. The power revealed in the life of Christ was becoming the authority of Christianity. A normal but perilous process was begun.

Authorizing Power

In the first generations after Jesus' death his followers made choices about celebrations and texts and customs that would both preserve the ideals of Jesus and define themselves as Christians. These beliefs and rules would give the Christian communities needed boundaries and identity: a process of self-definition was under way. In a movement that the sociologist Max Weber would call the "routinization of charism," and theologian David Power describes as "the canon-ization of power," Christians began to emphasize and safeguard certain patterns of power revealed in Jesus' life.

We describe this historical process, in which Christians today con-tinue to participate, as an *authorizing* movement: a series of deci-sions and judgments give birth both to a collective identity (as Christians) and to an authority (of Scripture, sacraments, canon law). This is a process that is at once necessary and dangerous. The authorizing process is necessary because the message and mission of Jesus survive among us, in part, because they have been "institu-tionalized" in this way. But the authorizing process is also perilous: the rules and roles that are "authorized" can take on a life of their own. When this happens the *process* of authorizing is replaced by a static "authority," seen as external to the community and indepen-dent of historical context. Authority goes into exile.

A first danger arises as a group attempts to define itself. An early sense of "who we are" comes from knowing "who we are not." This tendency to define self "over against" the other is a normal part of both personal and corporate maturing. By setting ourselves off from "those others" we see better the boundaries that tell us who *we* are. These boundaries, made manifest in our statements of belief and oaths of allegiance, add order and stability to the group's life. It is through these values and their protective structures that we come to a sense of identity as a group.

But there are risks. An emphasis on *certain* values entails the exclusion of others. To draw the line that clearly marks *these* books as Christian Scripture, we exclude other texts about the life and message of Jesus. In an effort to define *these* beliefs as genuinely Christian, we exclude other convictions. If this is normal in group life, it is especially dangerous in the world of religious values where "other" is so easily associated with what is unfaithful, heretical, even evil. In our own religious history, we know that efforts to define "the faithful" frequently result in increasing hostility toward others as "the infidel."

There is a second risk. Every authoritative action in the church—the deliberations of a council or the promulgation of a code of law —is "momentous," both as significant in itself and as bearing the limits of its own moment in history. These moments in the history of faith, once "authorized," tend to assume the guise of independence and immutability. The *results* of the process distract us from the importance of the process itself; previous decisions, interpreted now as God's unchanging will, mask the need for the community's continuing discernment of God's presence in its ongoing life. The community's participation in the authorizing process—that is, the daily decisions of a lively, practical faith—becomes neglected. Authority, now envisioned as both external and eternal, needs only to be obeyed.

The dangers that accompany the necessary process of authorizing power among us require a third stage of empowerment: purifying these patterns of power.

Purifying Power

The need for this third stage of empowerment arises from the threat inherent in every human structure: its tendency toward self-seriousness. Structures originally developed to safeguard and express our deepest values come gradually to replace any need for discernment. Authorized dogmas tend, in time, to substitute for religious encounter. Laws can seem to diminish the need for a continuing evaluation of a community's convictions.

The process of purifying patterns of power among us is intimately related to the role of symbols in human life. In the first stage of recognizing patterns of power, we forge metaphors to capture these values: a banquet meal, a driving out of obsessive spirits, the shepherding of a group. In the second stage of authorizing certain patterns of power, we generate images of leadership (father of the family; high priest at the altar) and of institutional life (a hierarchy). But these metaphors, however inspired, remain the result of human effort. God's revelation happens in and through these images, but they remain human vessels of grace. They may be, in certain periods, lively and suggestive. But they are also necessarily limited. Every metaphor limps. Every image has its shadow side, an aspect least likely to have been noticed by its originators. Over time the limitations of our authorized metaphors of community and leadership become more noticeable; their shadow side emerges and cap-

tures our attention. We are invited to the purifying of our patterns
of power.

The Christian tradition has tried to remain responsive to this
conviction by describing itself as *semper reformanda,* always in need
of reform. The process of this reform, a purifying of power, includes both memory and disbelief. Most often the purifying of one
authoritative structure is energized by the memory or recollection
of an ancient, alternative self-portrait. The stable and orderly image
of a city of God is altered by the recollection of the ancient and
mobile imagery of pilgrimage. We remain the people of God, but
now less settled and more agile. The conviction that the one correct
presentation of the Eucharist is as a thin white wafer (its officially
authorized form) is overcome by the memory of earlier celebrations using everyday bread. Reformers discover in their tradition's
origins long-forgotten themes and images. An amnesia of earlier
styles of leadership and of previous metaphors of community is
overcome by religious memories activated by change and crisis.

But for these remembered images successfully to challenge dominant metaphors of leadership and community, individuals and
groups must learn the difficult virtue of disbelief. As we will see in
Chapter Eleven, this paradoxical strength, which seems to threaten
the very survival of the group, in fact questions only certain self-
portraits. The virtue of disbelief does not deny God or the Christian tradition. It does challenge the adequacy of *specific* images and
rules. To allow the possibility of women liturgical leaders we need
to disbelieve previous assumptions about women's roles in the community. Since these assumptions have found expression and rein-
forcement in institutional statutes, it is here that disbelief is focused.
To permit the exciting image of a church as a mutually structured
community of shared decision-making, we need to disbelieve the
adequacy of our self-portrait as a hierarchical family. As a virtue,
this disbelief allows us to purify metaphors and structures that have
become unfaithful to a continually maturing faith.

EMPOWERING AND LEADING

This cycle of change and growth is one of empowerment: it generates and expands power in a group. "Empowerment" is a theme

that enjoys much attention in today's church. Energizing as the word itself is, it will flounder in rhetoric unless toughened by the virtues of personal maturity and skills of group intervention and change. Personal virtues help us recognize and contest our own temptations regarding power—whether these are to flee from it or cling to it. Group skills give concrete direction to our shared values and rescue Christian virtue from rhetoric.

Empowering as a collaborative process begins in the recognition of the flow and variety of powers among us. These powers will always be unequal: we have differing strengths and gifts. But these powers need not be imagined in a vertical fashion, as better and worse. Imagined in a more horizontal manner, we can picture our powers as *for* one another, instead of *over* each other. For a religious people, empowering is also rooted in the conviction that our power comes from the Spirit that moves among us, as it will. If power is neither an individual possession nor a privilege of a subgroup in the community, then empowering generates and distributes more power among us. As an exercise of religious generativity, we empower others by sharing our strengths and reminding them of their own gifts.

The three-stage cycle we are considering here suggests that empowering happens at each stage of a group's maturing. Max Weber's wonderful phrase, "the routinization of charism," may distract us from the variety of charisms needed for Christian leadership. Charism, in its deepest Christian sense, is not restricted to inventive and innovative leaders in the first stage of a group's life. Charism, as we saw in Chapter One, refers to the wide variety of powers available and necessary for a group's survival. In St. Paul's list of these gifts in his first letter to the Christians in Corinth (Chapter Twelve), these abilities range from healing to administration, from preaching to prophecy. Different aspects and different stages of a group's life call out various charisms and different styles of leadership.

In its beginning phase, a community profits from leaders gifted with imagination and with the ability to name the hopes of the group. Once established, a community especially needs leaders with administrative and other "ordering" gifts. In a period of crisis and renewal, communities desperately require leaders with the prophetic ability to see through the temptations of the status quo and envision alternate ways of sharing our deepest values.

Communities do not, of course, move through these three stages in a linear, logical fashion. Nor do they reside in only one stage at a time. Any complex group combines various needs of innovation, consolidation and renewal. A new community may thrive with the direction of an enthusiastic leader, but if it fails to organize and safeguard its best hopes in institutional form it will likely cease to exist. Another group may succeed at carefully organizing its strengths and values but may fail to purify and renew its institutions. Unpurified, such a community will begin to stagnate. Communities need a range of leadership abilities because they must continually recognize, authorize and purify their patterns of power.

The confidence of Christian faith prompts us to suspect that the variety of gifts necessary for our communities to flourish is already present to us. If we cannot recognize the innovators or organizers or reformers among us, it may be because we have learned not to see them. Our hope is that the following chapters will assist our recognition of the different gifts of service available and needed in today's church.

REFLECTIVE EXERCISE

In this chapter we begin our discussion of the necessary movement of a group through a cycle of empowerment. To help the movements of the cycle—from recognizing through authorizing toward purifying power—become more concrete, we ask you to reflect on a group that is important in your own life these days.

Select for this reflection a group with which you have some history. It may be a group at work or in your personal life, a community in the parish or in the larger world of your civic responsibility. Recall what you know about the group—its origins, significant events in its life since then, its most important values, the patterns of its everyday life. Spend some time in this recollection, letting your memories come alive again.

As you consider this group right now, where is it in the cycle of empowerment?

- Is it facing the challenges of getting started, *recognizing* its own power and purpose?

- Is the group at a later point, spending considerable energy in organizing its resources and attempting to preserve its best hopes by *authorizing* roles and rules?

- Is this group confronted by the need for renewal or reform, being invited in this way to *purify* its organizational life?

Be as concrete as you can, giving examples from your own experience of the group that support your response.

ADDITIONAL RESOURCES

An excellent reflection on Christian life as an experience of empowerment is provided in David Power's "Liturgy and Empowerment," in *Alternate Futures of Worship: Christian Leadership* edited by Michael Cowan (Liturgical Press, 1987). Power urges the reinterpretation of the sacraments as sharings of power within the central empowerment that is life in a community. For an exploration of the different faces of power, see Chapter 11, "Reimagining Personal Power," in our *Seasons of Strength* (Doubleday Image, 1986).

One example of the various efforts in the Catholic Church to pursue the ministry of empowerment is the Center of Concern in Washington, D.C. (3700 13th Street, N.E., 20017). This group is especially concerned with questions of social inequity, analyzing the societal and ecclesial structures that frustrate that social empowerment that we call the virtue of justice.

CHAPTER EIGHT

RECOGNIZING POWER: THE WITNESS OF JESUS

The two friends walk listlessly on the road home to Emmaus. Jesus has been killed two days before and they walk in shock and defeat, struggling to make sense of this traumatic event. As they move along the road they are joined by a stranger who asks what they are discussing. We are alerted that this is a story about recognition when this stranger is identified: "Jesus himself came up and walked by their side; but something prevented them from recognizing him" (Luke 24:15–16). This is to be a tale about faith—the peculiar ability to recognize that pattern of God's power manifest in Jesus Christ.

Downcast and disgruntled, the two disciples ask the "stranger" how he could be ignorant of an event that has all Jerusalem astir. When their new companion persists in his inquiry, they explain Jesus' death and their own disappointment and confusion. Some of their women friends have reported that Jesus' tomb is empty but no one has seen Jesus.

To this report of distress, the stranger gives a startling response: "You foolish men! So slow to believe the full message of the prophets." Their traveling companion then goes on to recall for them the patterns of events, from Moses and the prophets to Jesus Christ, in which God has continually been revealed. Jesus' suffering and death, they are made to see, fit a pattern that is ancient and holy. The stranger's eloquence compels them to see again this pattern of life through death, a pattern they had come to believe but, in the midst of this trauma, have forgotten.

As they reach Emmaus the stranger makes "as if to go on." But the two disciples persuade him to stay the evening with them. While they eat supper together, the stranger says a prayer over the bread and hands each of them a piece. "And their eyes were opened and they recognized him." For a second time in this story their eyes are opened: on the road they had been made to recognize the patterns of God's power in their history; now they are brought to recognize Jesus Christ in this prayerful, symbolic action of breaking bread together.

In the midst of this recognition, something else extraordinary happens: Jesus disappears. "But he had vanished from their sight." This sentence, which reminds us that this is a story of insight and revelation, has always disturbed some readers. Is not faith a stable, guaranteed presence of God? Yet here Jesus appears, "strangely," on the road, is suddenly recognized at supper and then is gone. What can such mercurial movement have to do with an abiding faith? One answer, as we shall suggest in a moment, will have to do with the link between faith and the imagination.

The disappearance of Jesus does not dishearten the two. Instead enthusiasm surges through them. " 'Did not our hearts burn within us as he talked to us on the road and explained the scriptures to us!' " That evening they return to Jerusalem to tell the others "what had happened on the road and how they had recognized him at the breaking of the bread."

This is a strange but wonderful tale of revelation and recognition. Jesus both recognizes the patterns of God's power in life and causes us to see them. And our recognition arrives at times like a stranger: it comes at unlikely times (a long walk in a mood of despair) and in unexpected places (a casual meal taken together). The appearance/disappearance of Jesus reminds us of the fragility of our religious vision. These patterns of power—whether it is the movement of life through death or the extraordinary nourishment available in a communal meal—are often strangers that go unacknowledged. The recognition of faith is not a physical vision, a hold on the obvious. It is a vision aided by the imagination. It requires a specially gifted imagination to recognize the patterns of God's saving power in human life. The data of history are, at best, ambiguous. Life through death, the possibility of forgiveness and hope: to recognize these patterns which are often enough less than patent requires a leap of the imagination.

Faith is an exercise of the imagination—not inventing a fictitious pattern or distorting reality's painful patterns but recognizing barely visible patterns of power. Christians have long been suspicious of the imagination because of its ties with sexual imagery and fantasies of rage. But the imagination is indispensable to faith: God's saving patterns of power are finally and practically revealed only when we recognize them, when we assertively seize the hints and clues strewn in our path and make of them a personal vocation of purpose and direction.

The fragility of the imagination also teaches us about the tentativeness of faith: now we see Christ, now we don't; now we recognize God's directive presence in our lives, now we seem to lose it. There is no cure for the fragility of faith. Our only strategy is to continually season our imaginations with the patterns of power which are repeated in the Scriptures: more and more familiar with the clues and hints of God's power, we train the imagination to expect the unexpected. Learning from the reversals and crises of our own life, we come to recognize how life arises through death. Seasoned by many long walks and communal meals, we come to be reliable companions of Jesus Christ and of one another. This story invites us to revisit the life of Jesus and its witness to God's power.

A WORLD OF POWER

Patterns of power, both creative and destructive, lie deeply imbedded in human affairs. The social milieu in which Jesus lived was, like ours, a network of power. As Jesus "grew in wisdom and grace" he became aware of the forces and energies that surrounded and penetrated this world: acts of affection and care forge bonds of trust; acts of injustice and violence raise walls of hatred; cultural customs and religious rules weave patterns of social power and authority. Jesus' genius lay in his response to each of these.

Before reflecting on his responses, it may be useful to recall the two common biases that Christians bring to any consideration of

Jesus and power. Many of us have learned that Jesus had nothing to do with power. Meek and humble of heart, he was thought to eschew this seemingly sinful part of human nature. The myriad stories in the gospels about Jesus' exercise of power make this bias difficult to sustain. A second bias pictures Jesus' power as "something" that he possesses; packets of this power are dispensed through his healing and preaching. As we have discussed in Part I, power is often envisioned as an entity that people carry within themselves. In the following pages we will try to counter this bias with a portrait of Jesus engaged in relationships of power: social interactions that range from creative to destructive to simply stagnant. Jesus became powerful for us as he celebrated creative forces, challenged destructive energies and ignored the stagnant powers in his world.

Justice

Jesus' recognition of three special patterns of power stands out: these are justice, nourishment and purpose. The society into which Jesus was born had long struggled with its ideals of social justice. Keen to establish a national identity over against hostile "others," the Israelites kept hearing their God challenge them to treat these "others" with rectitude and even mercy. God's injunction included the disadvantaged: orphans, widows, the destitute and also foreigners—those with alien languages, customs and religious habits. "You must not molest the stranger or oppress him, for you lived as strangers in the land of Egypt" (Exodus 22:21). Living justly was a pattern of social power that came to Israel as a command. But structuring a society in which justice could flourish, or even survive, was arduous. Other patterns of power—fear, exhaustion, bigotry—continually threatened Israel's holy ambition for justice. Throughout its history, prophets arose to recall the nation to this fragile pattern of social power.

In one of his first public actions, Jesus becomes a witness to this power of justice. "Jesus, with the power of the Spirit in him, returned to Galilee" (Luke 4:14). Coming back to the area in which he had grown up, he enters the synagogue on the Sabbath. During the liturgy he steps forward to read from the Scriptures. Unrolling a scroll of the prophet Isaiah, he reads a passage in which Yahweh demands justice for the poor and the suffering. "He has sent me to bring the good news to the poor, to proclaim liberty to captives and to the blind new sight . . ." (Luke 4:18). Putting down the scroll, Jesus announces "this text is being fulfilled today even as you listen" (4:21). He evokes this ancient power of justice out of the scroll into the social life of his time. His first preaching thus emphasizes justice as a pattern of God's power in life.

Recalling the pattern in Jewish history, Jesus encourages his hearers to remember this power and to allow its healing intrusions in their own society. In Mark's account, the people in the synagogue are astonished that, "unlike the scribes, he taught them with authority" (Mark 1:22). And it was a peculiar authority because it lacked the usual credentials. He was neither a rabbi nor a trained scholar of the Scriptures. Yet his preaching urged his hearers to renew their commitment to the pattern of power called justice.

Jesus' recognition of the power of justice was more than verbal. Beyond his preaching, his entire life exemplified the interplay of justice and mercy: he consorted with sinners, with women, with persons of questionable status. He displayed a special and continual interest in the infirm. He lived a simple, unostentatious life. Even louder than his words, his life witnessed to the power of justice. His recognition of this social pattern became, over a lifetime, an embodiment of this ideal.

Nourishment

A second pattern of power, embedded in human life and especially celebrated in Israel, is that of nourishment. In the distress of the desert the Israelites had been tempted to return to the comforts of slavery, with its pots of meat and garlic. In this hostile land they had come across manna—an unexpected source of nourishment. Special foods marked the many festivals in which Israel celebrated its bond with God.

Jesus seized this important part of Jewish life and gave it special recognition. He frequently gathered his friends and followers for a shared meal. (See, for example, Mark 6:30ff.) Eating with him reminded them that more than physical nourishment is involved when we take the time to eat together. More than the physical body is nurtured. The ordinary phenomenon of eating can take on an extraordinary power: when we take the time to eat together, we can allow our distractions to subside. A space and a mood open up in which we find the ability to forgive one another; we are refreshed in a way that cannot be accounted for in the food alone. In a communal meal the social body of a community is enriched and grows. But other forces play havoc with this nourishment. Other demands and pressures compel us to eat alone or "on the run" or to overeat. Unforgiven hurts and daily distractions conspire to block our return to a communal table. The power of nourishment is lost. Jesus' life celebrates and recalls an easily forgotten pattern of mutual refreshment and delight.

The gospels remember this more than caloric sustenance in the stories of Jesus multiplying a few fish and loaves of bread to nourish a large crowd. (See, for example, Luke 9:12ff.) In his final supper with his friends, Jesus both commemorated the ancient Passover and celebrated his coming death. The rich tradition of the Passover meal combined special food with the memory of God's saving actions for this people; at their last supper Jesus and his friends took the opportunity to taste the threat and grieve over the loss that awaited them. This meal and the others they had shared with Jesus had such an impact on his followers that they preserved and renewed the experience of communal nourishment in the sacrament of the Eucharist.

Purpose

A third pattern of power that shaped Jesus' world was an abiding sense of purpose. His people had learned about purpose slowly and painfully. In the desert they had believed, doggedly and often without much supporting evidence, in a promised land. Later, as captives in Babylon, they had hoped vigorously for rescue from their exile. Like any nation, or individual, they struggled to see the direction and meaning of life. They sought to recognize, in the myriad confusions of daily details, a pattern and a meaning. Often enough their lives, like ours, seemed an amalgam of happenstance and event that disclosed no special purpose; life appeared as a collection of random pieces of a puzzle that revealed no pattern. Then they would suddenly become aware of a plot—the journey was leading somewhere! These sufferings and detours were part of a larger design. Like justice and nourishment, this pattern is none too patent. Crises and failures made another argument. Periods of stagnation induced an amnesia of meaning. But when they again recalled their purpose the Israelites also recognized that it did not spring from their own resources. They recognized in this fragile ability to see purpose the power of their God.

As Jesus matured, he became aware of God's special purpose in his life. This purpose was tested in the desert where he was lured toward other uses of his life. Resisting these selfish purposes, he "returned to Galilee with the power of the Spirit in him" (Luke 4:14). As he became more attuned to his vocation, he invited others to join him and share a common life. The purpose that he constantly spoke of, that guided his own life, was an ambition called the Kingdom of God. This vision and purpose portrayed a world transformed by justice and love. It was a vision that lay at the core of Jewish life: from Abraham's search for a new home to the ex-slaves' desert journey toward a "promised land," Israelites had pursued a new and purified way of life. As with the patterns of justice and nourishment, Jesus gave special attention to this power, letting it shape his life.

The recognition of a special pattern of meaning in life Christians came to call a vocation. In reading the Scriptures today, Christians still hear invitations and intimations of purpose; they continue to be gifted with this pattern of power.

These three powers were not invented by Jesus; they were not "his." They already patterned the world in which he found himself. As his ancestors had, Jesus recognized these as gifts from the creator: justice, nourishment, purpose appear as half-hidden but inviting possibilities. Jesus' strength lay in his recognition and celebration of these special patterns of power.

Destructive Powers

But Jesus' recognition of power included more than these creative rhythms. Other patterns, especially of illness and compulsion, warped and ruined human lives. To these also he responded.

The gospels are filled with stories of Jesus' interactions with the ill and afflicted. The destructive powers of blindness, paralysis and infirmity repeatedly drew his attention. In Mark's gospel Jesus is constantly touching others in an effort to heal their wounds. In Chapter 8 of Mark we find an especially compelling example of this tactile healing: Jesus mixes his spit with some earth, rubs it into a blind person's eyes; gradually the person begins to see again. He is not afraid to touch a leper in order to heal him (Matthew 8:2–3). At other times this interaction initiates a more spiritual change: meeting with a woman caught in adultery, he first defends her from her self-righteous accusers and then encourages her to a more faithful life. His attention and empathy seem to excite her ability to change.

In one striking story we find the powerful, healing interaction of Jesus operating apart from his conscious control. Walking with his disciples through a dense crowd, he is approached by a chronically ill woman. Unable to get his attention, she reaches out and strokes his clothes as he passes. Jesus suddenly stops and asks who has touched him. His friends seem confused by the question since they have obviously touched many people as they jostled their way through the crowd. But Jesus adds: "I felt power flowing out of me" (Luke 8:46). In the Greek New Testament the word for power here is *dynamis,* the power of Yahweh. (In Latin the word is *virtus:* Jesus felt "virtue" flowing out of himself.) Touched in the right way, God's power moves through Jesus to heal others. Power is not in his possession. Instead, Jesus is the healing link between God's power and these wounded people.

Jesus' powerful interactions with others were often described as miracles. This notion, which strikes many contemporary readers as a kind of magic (the ability to multiply bread, calm storms and give sight to the blind), refers to profound changes taking place in persons who are in special touch with Jesus. It may be helpful to recall that the English word "miracle" is a translation of the same Greek word for power—*dynamis*. An English derivative of this Greek word for miracle is "dynamic": a miracle is a dynamic, a powerful interaction between people. In the English translation of the Jerusalem Bible this connection between miracle and power is made explicit. The people of Nazareth are astonished at Jesus' wisdom and "miraculous powers" (Matthew 13:54). Herod, hearing of his extraordinary actions, guessed that he might be John the Baptist come back to life "and that is why miraculous powers are at work in him" (Matthew 14:2).

One pattern of destructive power receives considerable attention in the gospels: the power of compulsion. In Jesus' world the force of compulsiveness was imaged as a possession: the domination of a person by some lethal power. The most dramatic account of this destructive pattern of power appears in the gospel stories of demoniacs or possessed persons. The frightening account in Mark's gospel tells this story:

> The man lived in the tombs and no one could secure him anymore, even with a chain; because he had often been secured with fetters and chains but had snapped the chains and broken the fetters, and no one had the strength to control him. All night and all day, among the tombs and in the mountains, he would howl and gash himself with stones (5:3–5).

This is clearly a story about power—a nameless power that inhabits a person, injuring him and driving him away from human society. Jesus confronts the destructive force in this person and compels it to depart. A crowd appears after this interaction and finds "the demoniac sitting there, clothed and in his full senses" (5:15).

Contemporary readers often edge uneasily around these stories that seem so primitive in their accounts of devils and possessions. To better glimpse the modern face of this destructive power it will help to recall the various compulsions and obsessions that "possess" us today in powerful ways. The most sensational example may be the aberrant patterns of habitual sex offenders, persons who seem driven to repeat acts of sexual violence, destroying their own lives as they inflict pain and even death on others. The defense of "innocent by reason of insanity" is another instance of the contemporary experience of possession: this plea rests on the argument that some alien force has compelled the individual to act in a destructive fashion.

Less sensational are the ordinary compulsions that warp and harm our own lives: compulsive habits of eating and drinking, or the "white-collar demon" that drives us obsessively after achievement and success. At different times we find ourselves gradually invaded or suddenly possessed with these "devils": we do not want to overeat, drink so much, work so competitively. But we feel driven, pulled repeatedly into behaviors that are destructive. Often, it seems, we cannot help ourselves. When we are delivered from these deadly powers—"exorcised" in the vocabulary of the New Testament—it is probably not by a churchly ritual but by the healing intervention of a friend, or lover, or therapist. This destructive pattern of power—compulsions and obsessions in both their daily and dramatic forms—awaits another pattern of power which challenges, confronts and drives it out. Jesus' life witnesses to a pattern of challenging and confronting these compulsions and obsessions. Following Jesus here begins in recognizing the contemporary guises of these ancient demons.

THE POWER STRUCTURE OF JEWISH LIFE

In addition to these "deep structures" of power—justice, purpose, compulsion—Jesus' world was also patterned by its social customs and religious laws. Jewish society, like any other, had constructed patterns of power and authority which defined and protected their shared heritage. These social structures extended from the temple with its priesthood to rules governing everyday interactions.

Detailed prescriptions limited one's behavior on the Sabbath; many actions were prohibited, such as the exertion involved in picking corn from the fields or interacting in a healing fashion with others. Aware of these rules, these persuasive patterns of social practice, Jesus chose to ignore some of them. While traveling, he deliberately ate the field corn with his disciples (Matthew 12); he healed a crippled woman and a man with dropsy, despite the rules that forbade such activity on the Sabbath (Luke 13 and 14). By no means an outlaw, Jesus chose to disobey some of the religious laws of his society. In this disobedience we see the crucial connection between recognizing and purifying patterns of power: emphasizing some patterns of power in a complex social world will likely entail the rejection of other patterns. Jesus' empathic intervention with the woman caught in adultery went against an established custom; it disobeyed an accepted pattern of social power. Recognizing certain patterns of power (empathy and healing) leads inevitably to purifying other patterns of power (social rules that encumber or discourage such care).

Within his cultural world Jesus neglected another powerful pattern of social custom: keeping a proper distance from women. He repeatedly ignored the religious and cultural etiquette about man/woman relationships. He conversed at length with a foreign woman at a roadside well, a woman to whom he had not even been properly introduced. He allowed a woman with a poor reputation to join his group at a meal, and even to touch him. Women were an important and intimate part of this unmarried man's group of friends. In strong contrast both to his cultural peers and to a subsequent clerical distancing from women, Jesus displayed a distinct familiarity with women. In so doing he was disobeying an established pattern of power.

Besides these cultural practices, Jesus also lived in a religious structure rooted in the temple and a cultic priesthood. How did he respond to these patterns of religious power? He certainly attended the synagogue and went to the temple. He did not reject this pillar of Jewish religious practice. But his life was such that his followers would, in time, recognize a radical reinterpretation of the temple and the priesthood. Jesus' own powerful interactions with others were, in fact, a purifying movement *within* Jewish life. Only several decades after his death would it begin to become clear that the energy and enthusiasm released by him could not be contained in a national religion. Christianity would become a world religion, embracing gentile as well as Jew, slave as well as free person. Circumcision would no longer circumscribe membership; kosher food would no longer describe Christian nourishment.

As the first generations of Christians looked back at Jesus' life (at a time when the gospels were being composed), they recognized something even more radical: the temple would not be a building in Jerusalem; it would be Christ's risen body. It would be wherever two or three believers were gathered together—whatever the housing or lack of it. The temple survives, but only in a radical reinterpretation. The ultimate sacrifice of a cultic priesthood had been accomplished in Jesus' death: in this final priestly act, priesthood was completed. "He has done this once and for all by offering himself" (Hebrews 7:27).

Henceforth, Christian leaders would bear the more secular titles of "elder" and "overseer." (Not until several centuries later would the metaphor of priesthood reemerge, as liturgy became more important in the community leader's role and as Christians sought to link themselves with their Jewish heritage.) In summary: Jesus recognized *within* Jewish life profound patterns of justice, community and healing; his followers recognized, in time, the implications of these insights: in *these* recognitions Christianity was born.

In this review of power in Jesus' life, we are developing a broader sense of recognizing. Recognizing patterns of power ranges from announcement to embodiment: Jesus preached God's benevolent powers of justice, nourishment and purpose, and his life came to embody these values. Recognition also includes a confrontation of destructive patterns of power, whatever the shape or current name of the possessive demons among us. Recognition even entails, it seems, neglect and disobedience. Jesus was not ignorant of the laws and customs that he ignored. To follow certain patterns of power is to neglect others—even some that are esteemed and sanctioned by one's culture and religion. This is the purifying edge of recognition: recognition leads to reformation. Finally, Jesus' different recognitions of power illustrate his various ministries—preaching justice, celebrating meals together, healing illness, prophesying new forms of power.

THE LIMITS OF POWER

Even the extraordinary power of Jesus learned the lessons of limitation. Repeatedly his interactions with others met barriers and restrictions that defeated his plans. A striking example of his power's limitation appears in an episode in Mark's gospel.

Again the story concerns Jesus' visit home and his preaching in the local synagogue. But in this recollection the people are not so impressed with his efforts and reject both him and his message. Jesus acknowledges the difficulty of succeeding with the home folk and utters the well-remembered phrase, "a prophet is only despised in his own country" (Mark 6:4). And then appears a sentence less well remembered: "and he could work no miracles there . . . he was amazed at their lack of faith" (6:5–6). Jesus' powerful interactions with others, both healing broken parts of their lives and leading them to recognize the patterns of God's power, depended on their acceptance and response. His ability to touch depended on others' willingness to be touched. Not an absolute power nor a secure personal possession, Jesus' power was an ability that depended on other forces to respond. The followers of Jesus would learn this painful lesson when, sent by him to preach and heal, they found they lacked the power to exorcise certain compulsions (Mark 9:14ff). This special dependency of Christ's power on others' faith —and of Christians on one another—has received too little attention in the study of religious leadership.

But a greater limitation on Jesus' power is especially celebrated in the fourth gospel. In this gospel we encounter a transcendent Jesus Christ, able to raise the dead and foresee his own coming death. We might expect a frequent use of the noun "power" *(dynamis)* in this account of his life. The word does not appear once. The verb "to be able to" or "to have the power to do" *(dynasthai)* does appear over twenty times in this gospel, nearly always with a negative nuance. "The Son of Man [Jesus] *can do nothing* by himself" (John 5:19). When a blind man, who has been healed by Jesus, is badgered by a crowd he retorts, "If this man were not from God he *could not do* a thing" (9:33). In his talk to his friends the night before his death, Jesus invokes the imagery of the vine and the branches: "cut off from me you *can do nothing*" (15:5). The negative grammar of this gospel insists again and again on a radical dependency of Christ's power on God: he has no power except what comes from God, and his followers will have no power except as they are connected with him. Christian power, far from being a personal possession, is doubly interdependent: it awaits the response and interaction of others, aware that a lack of faith and interest can defeat it. And it depends entirely on its source, the power of God.

The power of Jesus Christ, at once miraculous and dependent, shows yet another sign of limitation. It is sometimes reduced to powerlessness. The same Jesus whose power could touch and transform so many lives could not save himself. Failing to convince "the authorities" about the patterns of God's power at play among them, Jesus was killed in midlife. His power turned out to be, in a time of crisis, powerless. The paradox of this power failure is that his death generated a new style of religious living that would eventually bear the name Christianity. As the gospels carefully note, Jesus did not rise from the dead; "He was raised." The failure of his power was absorbed into a larger pattern of power. Thus did Jesus' life become a parable of power: human ability as dependent on a power that continually upsets our expectations about effectiveness and force.

CHRISTOLOGY—JESUS BECOMES POWER

Christology is the theological name for our efforts to answer the question "Who is Jesus Christ?" To provide an answer to this query, we need to explain this person's power: what was it, where did it come from, what was it for?

At times in our shared history, Christians have favored a portrait of Jesus as a God descending into human history, pretending—for our own good—to be one of us. In such a Christology, Jesus' power is fully divine, a resource he holds as a personal possession.

A quite different interpretation of Jesus Christ envisions him as a human person who grew in his ability to recognize the presence and power of God in life, until his own life finally embodied that recognition. His ability to represent God's power among us was so compelling that his followers saw him as more than a child of God. They (we) recognized him as the unique son of God.

To trace this growth in Jesus' life, and to glimpse how it generated a whole new religious way of life, we need to appreciate the full range of his ability to recognize power. This gift originates in the ability to see and acknowledge patterns of God's power at play amid the details and distractions of human life. But Jesus did more than spot these patterns; he announced them to others. In the synagogue, in conversations, in healing touches he gave these patterns a tangible shape; he made them believable.

The ability to recognize power matured in Jesus as the everyday actions of his life continuously witnessed to these patterns. His ability to trust (rather than get caught in frenzied activity on behalf of others), his insistence on prayer, his forgiveness and simple companionship made visible again and again God's presence and power. Unlike anyone before, his life became a convincing witness to God's power in human life. He came, finally, to embody the patterns of power that he preached: recognition had matured from acknowledging and announcing to embodiment. He was *becoming* the pattern of God's power. Eventually this embodiment would be named an "incarnation"—the enfleshing of God's presence and power in human life.

We are describing here what we have already seen in the Emmaus story: the man Jesus becoming the Christ; a human person becoming the enduring sign of God's grace in history. This is the movement from Jesus to Christianity, and from the first stage of recognizing power to a second stage of authorizing God's power in a specifically Christian way of life. The Emmaus story celebrates this passage from Jesus as a human sign of God's presence to Christ as the enduring (because no longer subject to death's intervention) embodiment of these patterns of power.

Paul, in his first letter to the Christians in Corinth, acknowledges this transition by referring to "Christ *who is the power* and the wisdom of God" (1:24). For Paul, Jesus no longer merely recognizes, or preaches, this power. He now *is* the power of God. As followers of Christ recognized how he embodied, incarnated, the patterns of God's power in human life, they became "Christians." They began to safeguard this revelation of God in Jesus by writing down their memories; some of these texts were later officially authorized by the Christian communities as Scripture. The first Christians began to establish rules and roles among themselves. They would before long formalize sacraments of breaking bread and forgiving and would develop names and rituals for ministers and leaders in the community. The stage of recognizing God's power, while still continuing, was being augmented and buttressed by a new stage of authorizing certain patterns of God's power: the Christian tradition was beginning.

REFLECTIVE EXERCISE

Recall the many gospel stories about Jesus' powerful interaction with others. Select one of these stories for reflection now. Prayerfully read the gospel account. Dwell with this story for some time, becoming present to it.

Consider these questions, spending time with the one that evokes the richest response.

What "pattern of power" does Jesus celebrate here?

What "recognition of power" does this story suggest in your own life?

To what "embodiment of God's power" are you called now?

Bring the reflection to a close, using Paul's words as a prayer of thanksgiving: Jesus Christ is the Power of God.

ADDITIONAL RESOURCES

Walter Wink studies the ambiguity of power in the New Testament in *Naming the Powers* (Fortress Press, 1984). Wink's interpretation of the "principalities and powers" language of the Scriptures is especially helpful in its suggestions of how these powers of human interaction become idolatrous and demonic.

European theologian Martin Hengel struggles with the Christian ambivalence toward power in *Christ and Power* (Fortress Press, 1977). Although troubled by a tendency to dichotomize holy and unholy power, and rational and extra-rational power, this book does further an important discussion.

In *Paul and Power* (Fortress Press, 1978), Bengt Holmberg studies the structure of authority in the early church as reflected in the Pauline epistles. The book is most useful in its analysis of Paul's own use of power. For an introduction to the language of power in the Christian Scriptures, one might examine Cyril Powell's *The Biblical Concept of Power* (Epworth, 1963).

Edward Schillebeeckx traces the movement from a "theology of Jesus" to a Christology in his *Jesus: An Experiment in Christology* (Random House, 1981). See especially pp. 545ff.

CHAPTER NINE

AUTHORIZING POWER: CHRISTIAN HISTORY

Jesus Christ led his friends and followers to see what lay before them: the patterns of God's power inscribed in human life. Jesus especially recognized and celebrated the patterns of justice, nourishment and purpose. But such powers, revealed in the life of Jesus, are most fragile and easily forgotten. So his followers determined to remember these patterns of power. Their memories would be preserved in the social structures of Scripture, liturgy and the institutions of our shared religious lives.

AUTHORIZING SCRIPTURE

The four gospels collected in the Christian New Testament are our recollections of Jesus' life. In these stories the power of his healing and of his challenge becomes available to anyone who would read them. New Testament letters, especially those of Paul, and other writings, such as Hebrews and the Book of Revelation, show how the first Christians understood God's action in Jesus Christ and applied it to their experience in the world. How subsequent generations of believers first assembled these records and then translated and interpreted them form a crucial part of the history of Christian authority.

In Christian piety, and sometimes even in theology, God was pictured as speaking the words and sentences of Scripture directly to individual writers, who—thus inspired—simply wrote what God dictated. Each word was literally "God's word" and an unambiguous revelation of God's power and purpose.

In recent decades scholars and educated Christians have become more comfortable with the recognition that God's revelation always finds expression through a *human process.* Inspiration, which simply means God's special guidance, is as extensive and diffuse as that process. God was present in the church's preaching, in its worship, in its teaching. God guided the young church through the Spirit and helped it maintain a living memory of Jesus' words and works. God gave the church the authority to keep Jesus in mind not as a touching memory from the past but as a living presence that allowed them to find new meaning in his life, death and resurrection, as they faced new concrete situations.

In the decades after the death of Jesus, various individuals and groups began to record their memories of Jesus' life and to exchange letters about their own efforts to follow his hopes and visions. Paul wrote most of his letters to various communities during the fifties of the first century, twenty to thirty years after Jesus' death. Mark's gospel, according to current scholarship, probably reached its final form between the years A.D. 65–70. The fourth gospel, a later product of a very different community of Christians, as theologian Raymond Brown has carefully shown, probably reached its final edition toward the end of the first century.

During the century after Jesus' death and resurrection, different accounts of his life and various letters were circulated and gradually became recognized as authentic and accurate to Christian memory and conviction. Pastoral letters, such as those to Timothy and Titus, and the second letter of Peter, were written to more developed communities, probably around the beginning of the second century.

As we learn about this process of transmitting, writing, editing and selecting, we recognize that some stories were left out of the final edition and some letters were rejected. Early documents, such as the *Gospel of Thomas* and the *Shepherd of Hermas,* were cherished in some Christian communities. But they would be excluded from the collection we call the New Testament.

A century after the death of Jesus there existed a splendid array of letters, gospels and other writings about Christian life. Certain of these were the preferred accounts of one region of Christianity while being hardly known in another geographic area. As the memory of Jesus' life grew more distant, new and different versions of his ministry competed for acceptance. A movement began to designate certain texts as central and authentic for all Christians. This effort to select a "canon" of texts was, in fact, a process of authorizing Scripture. Debates, disagreement and compromise during the first centuries of the Christian tradition led to the gradual establishment of certain texts as definitive and authoritative. This process both acknowledged the compelling force of these texts and with such recognition *gave them* authority over Christians.

In this chapter we are emphasizing the gradual, human process of acknowledging and designating where God's salvific power is found. To concentrate on the process of authorizing requires special effort. Traditional discussions of the authority of the canon of Scripture stress the *end product* of the process and often disguise the dynamics that originally produced the canon and that necessarily continue, in various translations and commentaries.

Abstract and static nouns, such as "canon" or "authority," easily create illusions about the ongoing process of authorizing. One illusion is that the canon of Scripture was simply given: a divine selection of certain texts was given to the Christian community apart from debate and decision. The canon of Scripture is then ascribed an authority unconnected with human responsibility and choice. In fact the community's tradition of faith preceded its canon of Scripture and served as the touchstone of Scripture's authority. But the community's faith had itself been shaped by the same documents that later were accepted as canonical. Scripture shaped the tradition, and the tradition helped shape the canon.

A second illusion associated with a static view of Scripture's authority is its univocity: the entire New Testament (and Hebrew Scriptures too, for that matter) is seen to convey a single message, unambiguous in every detail because it comes from a single, divine author without human interference. Here we can note again the connection between authors and authority. The *process* of selecting a canon of Christian Scripture celebrates our participation in the authority of these texts. Without reducing Scripture to a solely human

authorship, we can admit the unavoidable hazards of our historically transmitted tradition: every scribe, searching for the right
word or image to portray God's saving power, necessarily becomes
an interpreter and coauthor.

This second illusion also includes another suggestion: in a univo-
cal, unconflicted Scripture each part of the text would enjoy an
equal authority. Yet as pastoral experience indicates, this is not the
case. Christianity rejects most of the ritual laws of the Hebrew
Scripture, while accepting much else—the story and imagery of
creation, the ten commandments, the prophets' judgments about
social justice. In the New Testament the epistles to Timothy and
Titus do not enjoy the authority of the four gospels. This is true at
the personal level as well, as theologian David Tracy has suggested
in *The Analogical Imagination.* Each of us employs a "working
canon" of Scripture—favorite stories, evocative images, important
moral convictions to which we regularly return. We necessarily
favor some parts of our vast and rich Scripture, thus giving them a
special authority in our life. Such a preference entails the neglect of
other parts of Scripture—a practical amnesia, if you will.

A third illusion, arising from a static, abstract vocabulary, is that
the authority of Scripture is eternally fixed: it requires no continued
scrutiny from the community of believers. This view conveniently
forgets the diversity at the heart of these texts: documents which
record in Greek the life of an Aramaic-speaking Jesus; four different gospels composed over nearly a half century. The process of
authorizing Scripture, as the continuing discovery of truth and rele-
vance in these documents, reminds us of the importance of the
translations and commentaries in this lively, historical movement.
The history of the translation of the Scripture, as a part of this
authorizing process, may merit a moment's notice.

In the years 383–85 in Rome, Jerome produced a definitive and
authorized translation of the Bible. This translation from earlier
Greek texts made the Scriptures available to anyone who could
read Latin, the common language of the time. Jerome's translation
was appropriately named "the Vulgate"—for the common or "vulgar" reader. (The notion did not have the pejorative nuance that it
has today.) This Latin version became the standard edition of the
Bible in Europe for the next eleven hundred years.

The next major translation of the Bible was part of the revolution caused by the printing press. At the end of the fifteenth century there were two concerted efforts to reproduce the Bible in its original languages. In Spain, King Ferdinand and Queen Isabella sponsored a scholarly translation of the Scriptures. This extraordinary edition, called the *Biblia Poliglota Complutense* and printed in Hebrew, Greek and Latin, was finally published between 1514 and 1517. In 1516 the Renaissance scholar Erasmus published a new Greek and Latin edition of the New Testament. Both these efforts reminded Christians that Jerome's Latin text was not the exact words of Jesus but a translation in a particular cultural setting.

This enthusiasm for translating the Latin Bible *backward* (into its original tongues of Hebrew and Greek) accompanied a new ambition to translate it *forward*—into the vernaculars of Germany and England. Latin was still the official language of the regal and legal courts, but a burgeoning nationalism set the stage for translations into English and German. Although John Wycliffe's English translation of the New Testament had been available since 1384, the Protestant Reformation spurred new translations of the sacred text. Martin Luther's translation of the Bible into German in 1534, a version emphatically unauthorized by the Catholic Church, followed Tyndale's English translation of the New Testament, which appeared in 1525. The Christian Scripture was again being made available to the "vulgar," nonscholarly believer. Different nuances and new meanings (and the possibility of more believers recognizing these nuances and meanings) sprang from these novel versions of the Scripture; the perilous process of authorizing Scripture was continuing.

The Authority of Scripture

The patterns of God's saving power, recognized and embodied in Jesus Christ, are preserved and celebrated in the Christian Scriptures. By formally designating these texts as our canon, we give them authority in our lives. But, more specifically, what is the authority of these texts? In what does this authority consist? Historically, Christians tended to identify this authority as external: as God's word, Scripture comes to us as absolute truth and is to be obeyed. Questioning and interpretation have no place here, for this would be questioning the Scriptures' divine author.

Contemporary research on the nature of the "classics," a genre to which the Christian Scriptures belong, suggests a more internal source of the Bible's authority. The authority of Scripture resides in its ability to tell us who we are. As David Tracy demonstrates in *The Analogical Imagination,* this religious classic gives us our identity as humans and as followers of Jesus Christ. We find in it stories and images and paradoxes that resonate with those of our own life journey; and they more than match our lives, they illumine them. When we read the Scriptures in the midst of a crisis, or a delight, or while struggling to forgive someone, we find ourselves there. Jacob's wrestling with God is like our own; Jesus' distress the night before his death illumines our own dark nights. His ability to confront the demons of compulsion strengthens our resolve to do likewise. In these stories we are revealed to ourselves. We are empowered to believe our best ambitions. We are identified.

The process of authorizing Scripture finds its fruitfulness as these stories, in turn, authorize us to live according to the insights and values and paradoxes of the life of Jesus. This authority is practical and internal rather than external or abstract. And it does not always succeed. For various reasons, ranging from distraction to depression to anger, people may be ill disposed to recognize themselves in these stories. When they cannot find themselves there, we do not do well to insist on the Scriptures' external authority: "You must believe these books because they are God's word!" A more pastoral strategy, one that attempts to uncover the parallels between the rhythms of Scripture and a person's own life, will be more fruitful.

Another aspect of a classic is its endurance: it continues to reveal us to ourselves. We turn to it again and again for new soundings of our own unfathomable ways. Some stories we never tire of; we are like the child who begs, "Read it again!" As we continue to be revealed to ourselves, we are in turn authorized to live a certain kind of life. The authority of Scripture authorizes us to shape our lives according to certain patterns of power—justice, nourishment, purpose. And as we mature in these authoritative patterns of power we in turn empower others to follow similar paths.

AUTHORIZING CHRISTIAN MINISTRY

In the first generations of Christians after the death of Jesus there existed a rich and splendid confusion of ministries. Different members of these small communities found themselves gifted in healing or preaching or administration of their common resources. These communities gathered in someone's house to pray and share a meal in memory of Jesus; they informally divided the different tasks that arose—collecting funds for a widow or a poor family, confronting a member who was acting dishonestly or promiscuously, planning a celebration to commemorate some event in Jesus' life. Leadership in these "house churches" was derivative and subordinate to these services or ministries. As theologians such as Edward Schillebeeckx have shown, the first generations of Christians knew neither an elaborate structure of ministry nor a formalized leadership. Ignited by both an immediate memory of Jesus and a strong expectation of an imminent end of the world, these communities felt little need for formal organization.

As this religious movement expanded to new cultures and as an apocalyptic expectation of an end of the world waned, Christians began to feel the need for a more organized ministry. Caring for the poor had become a full-time job; preserving liturgical celebrations that were faithful to Christ's memory became more difficult as these rituals were influenced by the rites of other cults. Christians began the process, which still continues, of authorizing specific forms of ministry and leadership to meet the needs of the times. Turning to certain metaphors in the Scriptures (such as shepherd and servant) and borrowing other images from the surrounding culture (such as the titles of "elder" and "overseer"), Christian communities began to fashion a semiformal structure of ministry. We will explore this long and complex process of authorizing ministry and leadership by examining just two early movements: the coalescing of charisms and the evolution of presbyter into priest.

As we turn to this exploration, it may be useful to recall how a *process* of authorizing ministry challenges a still widespread but ahistorical picture of Christian beginnings. Many Catholics have been educated to a vision of an eternally present church ministry and its authority. In this portrait Jesus ordained the apostles as priests; Peter was installed as the first pope. The ministry of these first-generation clergy is seen as administering the seven sacraments to a lay faithful. A more historical view of our religious origins reminds us, first, that Jesus was emphatically *not* a priest—either in the then contemporary sense of a Jewish high priest or in the modern sense of ordained Catholic clergy. Those who led Christian communities during the first several hundred years were lay persons, since no vocabulary or distinction of clergy and lay had yet arisen. The patterns of ministry and leadership that we know now were not fully developed in the lifetime of Jesus. His extraordinary life generated an enthusiasm and commitment that gradually needed a formal, if changing, structure in order to preserve the patterns of power revealed in his life. As theologian Thomas O'Meara has so carefully demonstrated in *Theology of Ministry*, Christian ministry evolved as each generation of believers responded to new and different needs. The shape of Christian leadership continues to change today as the process of authorizing ministry moves forward.

The Coalescing of Charisms

The earliest communities of believers contained a variety of ministries and services, both enthusiastic and disorganized. As Paul suggests in his letter to the Corinthians, different gifts or charisms led to various services: preaching, administrating, prophesying, healing (I Corinthians 12). Before long, however, the Christian church began to expand rapidly and extensively. The need to coordinate a broadly spreading faith and to safeguard this fragile new church from heresy and misinterpretation led to the first formalizations of Christian ministry. The first names for formally recognized ministers were secular terms. Community leaders were called "elders" (or presbyters) and "overseers" (from which the name "bishop" derives). A third role and title, taken from the Scriptures, was that of deacon ("attendant"). Bishop, presbyter, deacon: gradually the wide variety of ministries—healing and preaching and prophesying and administering the community's resources—began to coalesce into these three roles of leadership.

From the second to the fifth centuries Christians increasingly expected the overseer or bishop to possess a whole range of ministerial gifts. With the expansion of Christianity in the third and fourth centuries, the bishop's role evolved from that of local pastor to become that of regional administrator. As this happened, elders stepped into the role of local community leader. Deacons were for a time active members of this leadership constellation, serving as delegates of the pastor in handling, for example, a community's practical questions of health care and finances. But the role of deacon quickly withered, along with the variety of different ministries in the community, as the community leader came to absorb into his role the whole range of ministries.

The coalescing of different charisms into a single leadership role (whether that of bishop or elder) culminated in the expectation that the local priest be "all things to all men." This gradual development had several intriguing features. First, it entailed the practical disappearance of the ministry of prophecy. The ancient and honorable ministry of the prophet, so much a part of Jewish tradition, was still very much alive in the time of Jesus. John the Baptist was called a prophet. Jesus' own ministry—as an itinerant preacher announcing the Kingdom of God—was a prophetic vocation. During the first hundred years after Jesus' death Christian prophets continued to thrive and contribute to this new faith. But as the other diverse ministries were coalescing into the role of bishop and elder, prophecy began to disappear.

A number of explanations have been offered for this absence. Developments in Christianity that were judged heretical, such as Montanism in the second and third centuries, emphasized the ministry of prophecy. (Not incidentally, that group's style of prophecy was often both ecstatic and exercised by women.) The rejection of such movements led to the neglect of this ministry. Another view emphasizes the natural antipathy between community administration and prophecy. In ancient Israel the prophet most often stood at the margin of the community, challenging both king and high priest—the central administrators of the group. Prophets in today's world—whether their name be Martin Luther King or Daniel Berrigan—continue to find their home at the edge of the culture. To be sure, some early bishops inherited this charism and continued to exercise the ministry of prophecy (as do some bishops today), but administrative leadership is not the natural habitat or most support-ive climate for this special gift.

A second feature of the coalescing of different ministries into the role of the bishop or presbyter was the development of a special image of the community's structure. This was the metaphor of hier-archy. Coalescing was envisioned as a gathering *up;* in a vertical image of community life, the elders or *over*seers were imaged as positioned over others. Leaders were lifted up in order to serve. Vertical images of society were strong in the cultural setting of early Christianity. Their religious heritage (the monarchy of Israel) and their cultural experience (the Roman Empire) reinforced this verti-cal image as a portrait of reality itself. In the fifth century a writer referred to as Pseudo-Dionysius introduced the word "hierarchy" into the church's discussion of ministry. In a time when this meta-phor of social life no longer enjoys a universal sanction as "the way reality is," we struggle to recall that a hierarchy is not divine revela-tion but a human metaphor. This image of social life is a historical artifact developed by our ancestors to authorize a specific structure of the Christian community.

A third, fateful movement within the coalescing of ministries into a single leadership role was the choice of metaphor to describe the leader. From among the many images available in their religious experience and cultural life, Christians early on began to emphasize the metaphor of *paterfamilias*—father of the household. This image of the leader was borrowed more from the cultural milieu of the Roman world than from Christian memory: Jesus had urged his followers to call no one "father." The special attraction of this metaphor, as we noted in Chapter Two, is its suggestion that the faith community is a family. In this image, the leader is urged to care for the community with the affection of a father. But, as theo-logian Elizabeth Fiorenza has amply illustrated in *In Memory of Her,* the image of *paterfamilias* carries other nuances that make it ques-tionable as a model for Christian leadership. In the Roman world a father of a household is an owner: his wife and children and slaves are his property. In such a hierarchical world, he stands above the community as not only father but ruler. The leadership of the *pater-familias* suffers the constant temptation of degenerating into pater-nalistic control. Over the centuries during which this metaphor of leadership has prevailed, Christian leaders have not always been successful in resisting the temptation.

These observations about the authorizing of structures of ministry are meant to remind us of the fragility and humanness of this process. Guided by God's presence and grace, we continue—often in trepidation and with hesitancy—to authorize new forms of ministry. The traditional self-designation of the church as *semper reformanda* (always to be reformed) reaffirms this fragility as it challenges the rigidity of past authorizations.

Presbyters Become Priests

A second major development in the process of authorizing structures of ministry was the transformation of the community leader into priest. Among the earliest titles for community leaders was that of "elder" or "presbyter." This secular name was used in various communities to describe a number of community leadership functions. During the third and fourth centuries these presbyters began to be described as priests. An enthusiasm for the Jewish imagery of the high priesthood was coupled with a changing vision of the Eucharist, seen now more as a ritual sacrifice than as a meal or banquet. Christians began to picture their leaders as priests, like the cultic officials who had served in the temple in Jerusalem before it was destroyed. The ritual and liturgical role of the community leader received greater attention. The single New Testament reference to Jesus as priest—in the letter to the Hebrews (7:27), where his priesthood was judged as unique, sufficient and unrepeatable—was invoked to authorize the new view of the leader.

Accompanying the evolution of the presbyter into priest were two other developments that would profoundly influence the shape of Christian ministry: leaders were becoming celibate and clergy. There appeared especially in the fourth century a growing concern that *all* community leaders assume a celibate life-style. This newly urgent concern had at least three historical roots: it was grounded in the memory of Jesus' unmarried status; it was related to the metaphor of the leader as priest (with suggestions of a special purity required for those handling a community's sacred rites); and it was powerfully shaped by a deep hostility toward sexuality prevalent during this century. This was the century when Manichaeism, with its repudiation of sexuality and the body, would influence such powerful leaders as Augustine and Jerome.

From the synod of Elvira in Spain in 309 to the synod of Carthage in North Africa in 390, married community leaders (priests) were being asked to abstain from sexual intercourse because of their priestly calling. For the first time the sacraments of priesthood and marriage seemed to be in conflict. Gradually celibacy replaced abstinence as the ordinary expectation (if often unmet) of formal ministry. In the Second Lateran Council of 1139, celibacy was finally and officially promulgated as a requirement for community leadership/priesthood. The process of authorizing structures of ministry had come a long way from the New Testament injunction that the bishop "be a person of irreproachable character, not married more than once . . ." (Titus 1:6). The contemporary challenge to celibacy as a requirement for community leadership does not question the *gift* of this life-style, which has continuously demonstrated its gracefulness and fruitfulness in Christian history. It does question the *bonding* of a specific life-style to the ministry of sacramental community leader. When we recognize that this connection is not an eternal union but the result of historical pastoral choices, we become authorized to bring under prayerful and communal review the connection between leadership and life-style.

During these same third and fourth centuries another important authorizing movement was under way. Christians began to distinguish their leaders as enjoying a separate social class. Borrowing a distinction from their cultural setting, Christians began to speak of "clergy" and "lay." Influenced by a society eager to distinguish different strata of excellence and privilege, the church defined its leaders as belonging to a special social status. This social difference, so foreign to Jesus' life and the mood of the New Testament, became more pronounced as the clergy adopted distinctive clothes. This development was, for a time, resisted by the church itself. In 428 Pope Celestine objected to another bishop's introduction of the special clothes of the monk: "We should be distinguished from others, not by our dress but by our knowledge; by our conversation, not by our manner of life."

The Exile of Leadership

All these changes—the leader as priest, as celibate, as cleric—led to the separation of the leader from the community. Socially distinct in a new status, the leader was also separated by his unique life-style of celibacy. The Eucharist continued to be interpreted less as a meal (with the leader sitting among others at a common table) and more as a sacrifice (the leader standing alone at an altar, now removed by reason of its sacredness). Church architecture reflected this distancing of the leader: the altar began to move from its more central location in the church toward one end of the building. The priest and the altar would soon be separated from the assembly, first by an altar railing, then by a curtain to be closed during the most sacred portions of the liturgy. By the sixth century the private Mass was becoming a custom: now the communal meal could be celebrated without a community. Not only was the leader being separated from the community, he was taking the Eucharist with him.

This exile of the community leader from the community was reinforced in another development that is especially germane to our reflection on power. In the course of Christian history the sacraments had developed as patterns of power from which Christians repeatedly drew life. The "power" of a sacrament was given a new interpretation as the historical process of authorizing leadership continued. As the Christian theology of ministry became more intensely focused on the liturgical role of the priest, it became increasingly divorced from a theology of the community. By the Lateran Councils of 1179 and 1215 the priestly ministry was firmly defined in terms of its ritual function: the celebration of the Eucharist, and the other sacraments, was a "power" that belonged uniquely to this ministry, apart from considerations of the community of faith.

Sacramental power was no longer envisioned as the interactions of nourishment, forgiving and healing that build a community of believers. Now it was pictured as the potency of specific rituals. And these rituals were the exclusive domain of the priest. From this unhappily distorted view of religious power as a possession rather than a mutually accountable interaction grew a variety of excesses:

the anomaly of the private Mass; a near-magical view of baptism as a power affecting individuals apart from any supporting community; a faith community as totally dependent for the celebration of its own sacramental life on the presence of a formally designated leader.

This concentration of power in the leader represents a final stage in the coalescing of charisms. A splendid diversity of gifts had been gathered up into the office of the formal leader. He was then gradually exiled from the community, taking with him these ministries. Christian communities lapsed into a deep passivity; with no internal resources, they were compelled to await external and paternal care. Conversely, enormous expectations surrounded the role of leader: he should be an excellent preacher, healer, administrator. On both sides an imbalance of power, a misinterpretation of the patterns of power revealed in Jesus, was becoming more apparent. Church historian Hans von Campenhausen raises the intriguing questions: Where did the various charisms once distributed throughout the community go, as they were replaced by the all-providing leader? Since a leader can be only so gifted, where did the surplus of energy and charism go? He speculates that they went underground. Deprived of having any influence on the community's life (since this was now handled by the formal leader), these energies and gifts sought expression in piety and in fervent, even magical devotions. Might there be a connection between the sometimes contorted forms of Christian piety and the formal location of all religious power in the role of the community leader?

Authorizing to Purifying

This exploration of the development of Christian ministry reminds us that it is both a continuing movement and a process that authorizes new forms of ministry. As successive generations of believers confront new challenges and opportunities they select new metaphors of community life, ministry and leadership. These choices give authority to new metaphors and authorize new versions of ancient patterns of power. When a religious tradition ceases this historical process it begins to stagnate. It clings to previous images and models of ministry, turning them into idols. Closing its eyes to new visions and revelations, it ironically authorizes its own demise.

If we learn anything from the witness of Christ we learn that life is a parable: our own plans are always being overthrown. This is the case not only in our personal lives but in our corporate efforts of ministry as well. Our best "authorizations" fall eventually under scrutiny and require purification. Metaphors that had once seemed so divinely inspired—our life together imaged as a hierarchy, our leaders pictured exclusively as male celibate clergy—reveal their shadow side. The authorizing of certain structures of ministry represents our best efforts to respond to the patterns of God's power that Jesus has recognized for us. But these efforts always await purifying. The reforms of the Second Vatican Council and the subsequent decades provide an excellent example of an effort to purify past authorizations of ministry and leadership. Our courage to continue this purifying process enables us to contribute to the ongoing cycle of empowerment that is Christian life in the world.

REFLECTIVE EXERCISE

In this chapter we have reflected on authorizing as a shared and continuous process. We invite you to explore how you practically contribute to the authority of the Christian faith.

What are your favorite passages or stories in the Christian Scriptures? Take some time to revisit their important and exciting images. Then recall how you may select one of these passages to read at a liturgy, or team meeting, or family prayer. When you do this, you *authorize* a specific text as a valuable resource for a group. You affirm its value in your life and reassert its authority. Are there important parts of the Scripture that you tend to ignore? Recall how such "forgetfulness" authorizes others also to neglect these passages.

A second area where we authorize a part of Christian life is in regard to ministry. Consider, for example, your own convictions about the involvement of lay persons in ministry. Whatever your belief, when you make it known to others you authorize *that* view of Christian ministry. If you judge that it is a question in which you have no say, then you authorize this lack of a contribution. What convictions about ministry do you authorize by your actions? Does this contribution, as an effort of authorizing, seem fruitful to you?

ADDITIONAL RESOURCES

Scripture scholars Eugene Ulrich and William Thompson discuss the historical processes by which the Hebrew and Christian Scriptures were produced in "The Tradition as a Resource in Theological Reflection—Scripture and the Minister," in *Method in Ministry,* by James D. Whitehead and Evelyn Eaton Whitehead (Winston-Seabury, 1981). In other work, Thompson offers a solid and practical orientation for those who wish to approach Scripture more confidently in their prayer: see his *The Gospels for Your Whole Life* (Winston Press, 1984) and *Paul and His Message for Life's Journey* (Paulist Press, 1986).

Harry Gamble reviews the current scholarly consensus on the gradual authorizing of those texts that would be called the New Testament in *The New Testament Canon* (Fortress Press, 1985). On the Christian Scriptures as a classic, see David Tracy's *The Analogical Imagination* (Crossroad Books, 1981) and Krister Stendahl's "The Bible as Classic and the Bible as Holy Scripture," *Journal of Biblical Literature* 103 (1984).

For some of the historical details in the authorizing of the first forms of Christian ministry, see David Power's "The Basis for Official Ministry in the Church," in *Official Ministry in a New Age,* edited by James Provost (Canon Law Society of America, 1981), and Elizabeth Schüssler Fiorenza's *In Memory of Her* (Crossroad Books, 1983). On the evolution of the presbyter into priest, see Chapter Four of James Mohler's *The Origin and Evolution of the Priesthood* (Alba House, 1970).

Representing recent efforts to re-evaluate authority in the early church and especially in the pivotal ministry of St. Paul is John

Howard Schütz's *Paul and Apostolic Authority* (Cambridge, 1975). Schütz studies authority as an interpretation of power and as the effort to "distribute and arrange the locus of power and more importantly, access to power" (pp. 13–14).

CHAPTER TEN

PURIFYING POWER: THE PRESENT CRISIS

When Pope John XXIII announced—on January 25, 1959—plans for a worldwide council, four hundred years had passed since the Council of Trent. The earlier council had been a response to the Protestant Reformation and arose in a profound crisis of authority. In the Council of Trent the Catholic Church defended itself against revolutionary notions of power and leadership, of ministry and liturgy. This effort of self-defense moved the church toward extreme positions on several issues of Christian life and service: ministry came to be understood exclusively in terms of priesthood; a focus on the ritual aspects of the sacraments distracted Catholics from the vital participation of the community in these rites; authority came to be pictured as belonging exclusively to clerical leaders, to the neglect of the personal authority of conscience. The eminent theologian Yves Congar has summarized this historical shift in the Catholic respect for conscience in his usual succinct manner: ". . . the condemnation of its abuse [in the Reformation] involved the end of its use."

In this time of severe crisis the Council of Trent had authorized certain patterns of religious power. At the end of the nineteenth century another council (Vatican I) responded to yet another crisis of authority. As Italy reclaimed the city of Rome as national rather than papal property, the church reasserted the special religious authority of its leader. Deprived of the Papal States, church officials were drawn to argue for the pope's infallibility. The political diminishment of the church seemed to increase its insistence on the absolute authority of its leader. These two councils—Trent and Vatican I —defined Catholic life through the first half of this century. The Second Vatican Council, with the rich and exciting hopes for Christian life that it generated, initiated a process of purifying earlier patterns of power and authority.

The movement that Pope John XXIII described as an *aggiornamento* (updating) was, in fact, a process of purifying patterns of power. This process is deeply traditional; it draws on the riches of our communal memory. We return to ancient but forgotten images of our life with God. The purpose is not to reject recent patterns as simply wrong or misguided; instead the community seeks the images that will help it overcome the partial and now limiting expressions of the past and reenvision, faithfully, the present demands of its life with God. Seeing, from the vantage point of the present, the necessary limitations of earlier images of faith, the council recalled and recognized alternative ways to authorize Christian life. The process of purification was again under way, in a faith community that acknowledges its continuing need for reform *(semper reformanda)*.

In purifying patterns of power we *recognize* again how God is among us; and in rerecognizing ancient but forgotten images, we *authorize* their contemporary influence in our lives. In this chapter we will trace this purification of power—a movement that is very much alive in the church today—in regard to the meaning of faith, the structure of the church, the shape of ministry and the understanding of the sacraments.

A PROCESS OF PURIFICATION

In the last quarter century a venerable image of religious experience has reappeared: faith as a journey. This image, which suggests both the flexibility and the fragility of faith, is rooted in our memory of our ancestors wandering through the Sinai Desert in search of a homeland. For the past three thousand years Jews and Christians have vacillated between two compelling metaphors of religious faith. These are the images of a journey and a state. Is faith a place to inhabit or a mode of travel? Is it a habitat, a secure institution in which to abide, or a style of search? It is, of course, both, our religious lives being too complex to be captured in a single, sufficient metaphor.

The oscillation between the images of journey and state describes the history of Jews and Christians. Settled into a new homeland, the Israelites under their kings David and Solomon seemed to have come into possession of a "promised land." But social injustices and other sinfulness put them on the road again. They were led into exile in Babylon. Similarly, by the middle decades of this century American Catholics had settled into a stable, even rigid institution of faith: clarity, order, secure boundaries protected our "state of grace." In the 1960s many Catholics felt the tremors in their once firm institution and heard the call to become pilgrims again. New invitations and demands lured us from our too secure habitat. For many this first, frightening movement felt like a dislocation. To Catholics accustomed to familiar ways—the regularity of Sunday Mass and Friday abstinence, the security of the large parish plant, the certainty of uncontested articles of faith—it came as painful news that their faith demanded movement. Long-unused muscles protested as the body Catholic stirred to take up the journey.

The recovery, and so the reauthorizing, of the metaphor of Christian faith as a journey brought us in touch with two half-forgotten convictions. First, God's revelation is never concluded; the plan of salvation unfolds as we continue to be revealed to ourselves. All the Christian dreams have not already been dreamed. The church has yet to fully imagine what God has in store for us. But if God's revelation continues, we must be faithful to both past and present insights. God continues to speak—encouraging, confusing, surprising us. As this conversation continues, we need to be alert and agile. In a time of crisis and transition, the metaphor of journey is again authorized as a fruitful self-description of the community of faith.

Second, faith is experienced not as a possession but as a resource for this journey. Faith is recognized not as a jewel to be guarded and defended within institutional boundaries but a surprising presence we stumble onto in our travels. To some this must feel like a diminishment: faith is robbed of its sureness and strength; it loses its quality as a guarantee. Indeed, faith does become more fragile, even a "sometime power," for we find at times we cannot summon or produce it. But in this metaphor our understanding of faith becomes more like our experience. The image of faith as a journey more adequately describes our movement with and toward God. Thus a reimagining of faith becomes an exercise in purification.

THE CHURCH

The process of purifying patterns of power has also touched the church's image of itself. A pervasive and dominant self-image of the church as a hierarchy is now being challenged by the equally ancient metaphor of the Christian community as a place of radical mutuality.

In the prevailing metaphor of hierarchy, the community of believers was pictured in a vertical fashion: different strata of Christians (laity, vowed religious, priests, bishops) composed a pyramid of ascending excellence and authority. Within the clergy itself various ranks had developed: pastors, monsignors, bishops, archbishops, cardinals. For centuries we had pictured ourselves in a metaphor which seemed to mirror reality itself: royalty were superior to freemen who were above slaves; husbands belonged above wives who were above children; a religious cosmology echoed this reality with its own realms of heaven, earth and hell.

The strengths of the metaphor were order and clarity. We each knew where we belonged. And we did belong: this hierarchy was one of affection and care, as well as one of power and privilege. For many centuries an effective ministry was exercised in this model of the church. Such a self-portrait also envisaged a clear chain of command: upper echelons of the clergy directed local pastors who instructed the docile faithful.

The first generations of Christians, influenced by the hierarchical world that surrounded them on every side, structured their communities and ministry according to this image. Privileged memories of Jesus' life and values were shaped into authoritative structures of ministry and leadership. Our ancestors were, in our vocabulary, authorizing certain patterns of power. Gradually, hierarchy as a self-portrait gained a pervasive authority among us. And, as with every metaphor, the success of this image fostered an amnesia of alternative portraits of the church. In the deliberations of the Second Vatican Council, one of these almost forgotten images returned to our shared memory with a powerful impact.

The metaphor of the church as a place of radical mutuality, revolutionary as it is, is neither an invention of modern liberals nor a borrowing from cultural theories of egalitarianism. This ancient if often forgotten metaphor of the church is firmly rooted in the New Testament. Perhaps its most radical expression is found in the Pauline letter to the Christians in Galatia (in present-day Turkey). Paul reminds the believers there that their baptism has introduced them into a oneness with Christ. This unity is so exceptional that it shatters every distinction of race, gender and political privilege:

All baptized in Christ, you have all clothed yourselves in Christ, and there are no more distinctions between Jew and Greek, slave and free, male and female, but you are all one in Christ Jesus (3:27–28).

Such a portrait is shocking in a church dichotomized between clergy and laity, women and men. This image of a radical mutuality is so startling that not a few scholars have urged that it be interpreted as a vision of a future life, rather than as a practical imperative for Christian communities. If this ancient image jars us, it also recalls Jesus' instruction on the style of leadership appropriate for his followers. As we saw in Chapter One, in Matthew's gospel Jesus prohibits any vocabulary of status that would elevate the leader above others: titles such as "teacher, rabbi, father" are not to be given to Christian leaders (Matthew 23). The radical mutuality of the Christian life objects to such elitism, "for you are all brothers." Or, as theologian Elizabeth Fiorenza translates this phrase in her illuminating discussion of the passage, "you are all siblings."

In Vatican II Christians began to recall this ancient metaphor of radical mutuality to our collective memory. New vocabulary arose: collegiality, shared decision-making, team ministry. Even the pope, formerly isolated as the utterly unique leader in the church, was welcomed into a collegiality of bishops. His title of "bishop of Rome" was remembered, reminding us that he is one of our bishops as well as our pope. With much hesitancy we began to imagine our leaders and church structures differently. Religious congregations worked toward practical procedures for communal discernment and shared decision-making. Teams of ministers developed, struggling to collaborate in new and less hierarchical ways. Parish councils were established, inviting lay Christians to participate more authoritatively in the management of the local church.

As we looked around the community of faith, we found ourselves arrayed (sometimes, at least) in a more horizontal fashion. We were *beside* one another in faith and service, rather than above or below one another. In congregations of vowed religious, often the prophetic edge of ecclesial change, the vocabulary of leadership began to change. "Father superior" and "mother general" were replaced with less parental and more collegial titles. Change was often slower in diocesan settings: ministry teams including laity, women and men religious and priests were often officially ignored; priests retained the title of "father," complicating the movement toward a shared ministry of religious siblings.

As this metaphor of mutuality, at once ancient and novel, challenged and began to purify more hierarchical patterns of power, a profound ambivalence arose. Are we a people of mutuality or of hierarchy? This ambivalence is perhaps most sharply exemplified in the council statements themselves. In the important document on the church, often named by its opening words, *Lumen Gentium,* two very different images of the church are presented. In Chapters Two (The People of God) and Four (The Laity) a mood and vocabulary of mutuality prevail. In Chapter Three (The Hierarchical Structure of the Church) a vertical world view and a more juridical tone predominate.

In the exciting turmoil of the Second Vatican Council another ancient image of the church was retrieved and began to contribute again to a purifying of power: the image of the church as sinful. This image, as old as the Hebrew poetry depicting the faith community as an unfaithful spouse, seemed to need the metaphor of mutuality to encourage its own recovery. Arrayed hierarchically, we tend to protect our turf and status. The admission of our sinfulness becomes even more difficult than usual. When we picture ourselves more horizontally, beside one another, it becomes more permissible to share our weakness and sinfulness and to seek reconciliation. Priests, burdened in a hierarchical world with representing the sinless Lord, were expected not to be weak (or, at least, not to let it show). As the "teaching church" was sharply distinguished from the rest of the community, it became more difficult for this part of the community to admit error.

In the long historical process of authorizing certain images of the church, we had come to picture it as a sacred repository, the spotless house of God. The brilliance of this partly true picture hid other, more human aspects of church life. It disguised the sinfulness of a church inhabited by sinners and led to a neglect of the continual need for repentance. An enduring anti-Semitism, the excesses of the Inquisition and other more ordinary forms of malpractice became embarrassments to be denied rather than sins to be confessed. As we become more comfortable with the church as both sinful and grace-filled, we also come closer to one another. We can allow the promise of mutuality to dissolve ungraceful divisions between clergy and lay, and between women and men. In a climate of mutuality we can more easily admit our common sinfulness and can afford the special intimacy of caring for one another's wounds. Thus we continue the process of purifying power and authority among us.

MINISTRY

The process of purifying power initiated in Vatican II is a process of memory and imagination. Christians are recalling ancient, alternative images of how to be together and how practically to express their faith. Such a renewal will have a significant impact on Christian ministry.

Since Vatican II more Christians have remembered an old conviction: the call to ministry is rooted in our baptism. Welcomed into Christian life—whether as an infant or an adult—we are invited to express our religious hopes and values practically. As Catholics we are coming to reunderstand ministry as our baptismal faith overflowing into service. This may be the service of a priest or other professional minister; equally it may be the service given in one's career or civic community or family.

This imaginative broadening of Christian service challenges two earlier attitudes about ministry: the notion that ministry was an elite calling reserved to those with a special vocation; and that ministry was exercised exclusively *in* the church, as a sacred realm, rather than in the activities of the "secular" world. If Christian ministry is rooted in baptism, then all maturing believers are called to express their faith in action; everyone has a vocation that includes a witness to Christian values and service to others. The long-standing but ultimately unchristian distinction of sacred and profane has become an unfruitful way to imagine Christian life. Describing such a boundary between the holy and secular now serves less to focus our attention on God (its original intent) and more to restrict God's presence. God's presence *in* the church, and in the sacraments, and in the sanctuary, ought not to suggest an absence or deprivation of God beyond these locales.

By purifying the established patterns—the ways we have imagined and defined God's power among us—we begin to picture Christian ministry in broader, more inclusive ways. Rooted in a common baptism, ministry is portrayed as a shared imperative. As the common responsibility of a faith community, ministry becomes a more mutual enterprise. The differences among us in ministerial callings arise not from the presence or absence of a "real" vocation but from the specific gifts we find among us. Christians are not all called to the same ministry: pastoral ministry in a suburban parish differs from the calling to witness to one's faith through civil disobedience to protest social injustice. A ministry of caring for the terminally ill differs from that of teaching grammar school children. But these differences, which suggest both the shape of a vocation and the mode of our service, are more related to gifts than to lifestyle (married, single or celibate). These differences indicate a variety of function rather than of excellence; in a less hierarchical church, ministry is portrayed more as mutual service and less as a status occupation.

Once the special pattern of power that we call Christian ministry is broken out of a hierarchical world view, we recognize another feature of Christian service. Ministry is not meant to be *delivered* to a passive and docile community of believers. Ministry arises from within the community itself. Each faith community is recognized as a *source* of ministry, not just its recipient. Communities had always been generative of service, but a theology of ministry that emphasized a hierarchical world, in which only those officially authorized were named ministers and priests, led eventually to very passive expectations of Christian communities. As the vertical world of hierarchy is transformed into a more horizontal world of mutuality, the rigid distinction between "official ministry" and the diverse and ongoing service of other mature Christians begins to fade. (That this distinction still thrives in some circles is clear from the text of the 1976 statement of the Vatican on the (non) ordination of women: the document refers to priesthood as "ministry *in the true sense.*") Distinctions that protect status and privilege even while they separate different tasks in the community become less convincing. In all this, official ministry and leadership are being led out of exile, back into the community of faith.

THE SACRAMENTS

As the followers of Jesus reflected on his life they came to identify various patterns of power embodied there. Two of these patterns made a special impact on their memory and would lead to the development of the Christian sacraments. A first pattern concerned the daily needs of nourishment and reconciliation. As we explored in Chapter Eight, meals taken with Jesus provided more than food; in these communal settings, other needs, as human if not as physical, were admitted and satisfied. When they gave time and attention to their meals with Jesus, his companions were nourished in affection, consolation and confidence. In the intimacy of this sharing they found the opportunity to face their wounds and acknowledge their best hopes.

This pattern of mutual nourishment reached its unforgettable climax in Jesus' last meal with his friends. Quite naturally, Christians gathered often after that to break bread and share the nourishment of their food and compelling memories. God's power seemed especially present in these meals. Gradually the name "Eucharist"—thanks-giving—was given to this common meal taken in Jesus' name. A century after his death their meal had come to be a regular Sunday celebration.

Complementary to the daily need for food was that of forgiveness and reconciliation. Everyday hurts and larger wounds accumulate in any community. Finding the capacity to forgive and to ask forgiveness can be as difficult as finding food. Jesus urged his friends to forgive each other and encouraged them to ask forgiveness from God. Jesus even assumed the alarming authority to forgive in God's name. And he promised his followers that their mutual reconciliations would evoke God's forgiveness. This power to forgive, so fragile and elusive, demanded a ritual or practice in which it might survive. In the generations after Jesus Christians gradually formulated a sacrament of reconciliation—a ritual acknowledgment of our sinfulness and a petition for God's forgiveness. Christian communities developed and *authorized* this sacramental ritual to safeguard and preserve the power of forgiveness.

The other sacraments developed from patterns of power that followed a different rhythm. The rhythm of nourishment and forgiveness is a daily one: thus the repeatedly celebrated sacraments of the Eucharist and Reconciliation. A different rhythm appears in the several critical transitions that are inscribed into human life. One does not have to be Christian to recognize the importance of birth, marriage, illness and death. But Christians saw in these important transitions the likelihood of God's advent and grace. Jesus' own public life had begun with a baptism: John the Baptist had marked Jesus with water and a blessing as Jesus began his public witness to God's power. Influenced by this memory and by the initiation rites of other cults, Christians devised a sacrament of baptism to mark the entry of a new believer into the community of Jesus. Ceremonies and religious celebrations also surrounded Jewish marriages and funerals. From these clues Christians would, over many centuries, develop rituals to celebrate the passages of marital commitment and mortal illness. As questions of ministry became more complicated, Christians developed ceremonies and titles to mark the entry into community leadership. In a rite of ordination, neighboring bishops laid hands on the new leader who had been selected by a local community.

Traditionally Christians have often been encouraged to imagine Jesus explicitly and formally "instituting" the seven sacraments. This pious but ahistorical view of these patterns of power disguises the long process of Christian authorizing of the sacraments. The authorizing of the sacraments—the development of rituals and their rationales over many centuries—is rooted in the shared memory of Jesus' recognition of certain patterns of power in life. This authorizing was and is still performed by various communities as they seek to safeguard and revitalize Jesus' revelation of these rhythms of power. We participate in this authorizing process when we reenact the sacraments: our celebration reaffirms these patterns of power; our faithful revision of these rites both purifies and reauthorizes these rhythms of grace in human life.

But over the centuries this continual process of authorizing the sacraments receded from view. The sacraments came to be pictured as eternal, unchangeable rituals. They also came to be imagined as the sole province of the priest. He, and he alone in the community, "offered Mass," heard confessions and performed marriages. Today we are recovering a "forgotten" aspect of the sacraments: that each involves a process as well as a ritual; that each is performed by a community as surely as by an individual minister. To imagine the sacraments as the unique domain of the priest leads to a concentration on the ritual aspect of the sacrament and to a neglect of the contribution of the community.

In such a vision of the sacraments, a priest could baptize infants with little concern for the ongoing process—which only a believing community can effect—that practically and gradually inducts these children into Christian life. This arduous process of affection and education seemed accomplished in the ritual itself: the overburdening of the sacramental ritual gave it an almost magical cast. The potency of the rite itself seemed to relieve the community of its responsibility. A similar narrowing happened with the Eucharist: this sacrament came to be pictured as essentially the action of the priest. The community's participation continued to dwindle. By the sixth century the "private Mass" had appeared: this central celebration of the Christian community was taking the appearance of a personal devotion.

Since Vatican II our changing vocabulary and practice show a new vision of the sacraments. Today we speak of "the community celebrating the Eucharist" instead of the priest "saying Mass." The new rite of Christian initiation of adults emphasizes the community's role in sponsorship and witness. We are remembering that the couple itself is the minister of matrimony, not the priest; and we are beginning to recognize the role of other married persons in the community in the preparation of those approaching this sacrament. The Christian community is recognizing its role not only as the recipient of the sacraments but as the co-minister of the sacraments. Here too we are reimagining and purifying the power that is Christian ministry.

For many Catholics the impact of Vatican II was most emphatically experienced in the liturgy. In this weekly public arena they had grown accustomed to a very specific style of prayer and interaction. Then, suddenly, it all seemed to change. What was for many a breath of fresh air was, for others, a loss and a threat of unfaithfulness.

The church's living memory had come to imagine the Eucharistic liturgy in one unchanging way: the Mass as sacrifice; the bread as a wafer; the language Latin; the garments of the celebrant ornate and ancient. As we noted in Chapter One, research into our religious origins, reaching its maturity especially in Europe during the 1950s, made available to our shared imagination very different and even more traditional modes of celebration: the Eucharist as a banquet meal; the bread as an ordinary loaf; the language as the vernacular; no especially ornate or distinct garment for the presider.

These new possibilities supported a more crucial recovery: the community's participation in the liturgy. With dramatic impact, the altar was turned around and moved toward the congregation. Suddenly the community and celebrant were face to face at a common meal, instead of both facing an altar of sacrifice. With the liturgy now in English, it became necessarily more communal: the readings and prayers, in the vernacular, interrupted private devotions and drew us toward a more explicit sharing.

The enduring power of the liturgy was being altered; our patterns of interaction, with one another and with God, were being reshaped. The church itself was authorizing these changes, though this did not make the "tampering with tradition" less threatening for some. The church, having previously authorized certain patterns of celebrating the Eucharist, was now authorizing novel yet ancient patterns of celebration. Complementing this official reform were other stirrings in the church. We will explore these efforts of purification in the next chapter's discussion of the powers of the weak.

REFLECTIVE EXERCISE

Images of both hierarchy and mutuality are part of the community of faith today. Consider how this is so for you. Recall your own participation in the life of the church over the last several years—in the parish, in ministry, in the diocese and elsewhere. Spend some time with these memories, savoring both the events and the feelings that were involved.

Then identify among these memories a situation or setting in which the image of hierarchy was strong. What did you sense to be the strengths of hierarchy here, its contribution to the community of faith? What were its limits?

Next, identify a setting or situation in which the image of mutuality was strong. What, for you, was positive for the community of faith in this experience of mutuality? What did you see as negative?

Finally, consider a group in the church in which you participate regularly—a parish committee, a ministry team, a residential community, etc. Find examples that help you reflect concretely on these questions: What is the balance between hierarchy and mutuality in the life of this group? To what purification of power do you judge the group is being called?

ADDITIONAL RESOURCES

For Yves Congar's judgment on the loss of emphasis on personal conscience in Catholic theology, see his excellent article, "The Historical Development of Authority in the Church: Points for Christian Reflection," in *Problems of Authority,* edited by John Todd (Helicon, 1962), p. 143.

Perhaps the most influential book on the changing sense of the church has been Avery Dulles' *Models of the Church* (Doubleday, 1974). The purification of Christian ministry is being assisted by resources such as Edward Schillebeeckx's *The Church with a Human Face* (Crossroad Books, 1985).

Theologian Letty Russell explores the gospel challenge of radical mutuality in *The Future of Partnership* (Westminster Press, 1979) and *Growth in Partnership* (Westminster Press, 1981). For further discussion of a more robust theology of vocation, see our *Seasons of Strength: New Visions of Adult Christian Maturing* (Doubleday Image, 1986).

There has been an explosion of literature on the sacraments in the past decade. Examples of this fruitful reevaluation are Bernard Cooke's *Sacraments and Sacramentality* (Twenty-Third Publications, 1983), Joseph Martos' *Doors to the Sacred* (Doubleday, 1981), and George Worgul's *From Magic to Metaphor* (Paulist Press, 1980). Also see Tad Guzie's excellent *Jesus and the Eucharist* (Paulist Press, 1974).

CHAPTER ELEVEN

POWERS OF THE STRONG; POWERS OF THE WEAK

The purifying of church structures begun in Vatican II was largely a top-down reform. Bishops listened to the hopes and demands being voiced in Christian communities around the world. They consulted theologians, educating themselves in the best research on the history of Scripture, liturgy and ministry. Then, from their leadership positions in a hierarchical church, they began to forge guidelines and legislation for a purification of our Catholic way of life.

At the same time there was ferment from below. Lay people were coming to a renewed sense of conscience; women experienced the call to a more assertive participation in faith; parish priests were working toward more collegial relationships with diocesan officials. Maturing adults at all levels of this hierarchical arrangement keenly felt the incongruity of structures that rigidly dichotomized the followers of Jesus into shepherd and flock, leader and led, clergy and laity. The continuing promise of this ongoing reform is that so many of us in the church have the same goal: an adult church functioning through more collegial structures; a faith community distinguished by differences in gifts and responsibilities rather than divided by status and privilege.

In the hierarchical world which still describes our church structures, purification needs to be pursued both from "above" and from "below." Our strategies in working toward effective reform will differ, depending on our location in the structure. But our efforts have a common goal—to rescue leadership from its exile and return it to the community of faith.

STRATEGIES OF PURIFICATION

In the proper use of power, the giving and receiving go both ways —this insight guides effective institutional reform. As we saw in Chapter Three, the process of social power is reciprocal: it is in the *give-and-take* of our relationships that we are empowered as a group. Group structures must respect this reciprocity. Our images of authority must "tell the truth," acknowledging the give-and-take of social power. Our patterns of leadership must "do the truth," supporting the mutual accountability that keeps reciprocity alive. When institutional structures no longer express the give-and-take of power they stand in need of purification.

How is such structural reform to be accomplished? Action can be initiated both from "above" and from "below." Leaders can take steps to strengthen the give-and-take of social power. This is top-down reform, initiated by those in higher positions in the organizational structure. We will consider here several examples of institutional purification that originate "at the top," in the actions of those in leadership positions. Then we will look at efforts of reform that are generated from "below," in the actions of other members of the group.

Leaders make an essential contribution to the reform of structures when they use their power for the common good rather than for personal advantage. Holding themselves accountable to the words and witness of Jesus, they function among us as those who come to serve rather than to be served. When they act in this way, our religious leaders witness to a transformation of power that stands as a model for us all.

But for our institutions to be well ordered the exercise of power must not depend simply on the ethical sensitivity of those in charge. The give-and-take of social power must be safeguarded by social structures that go beyond the good will of particular leaders. There must be procedures that guarantee a lively dialogue between the group and its leaders. There need to be policies that hold leaders accountable in their relationship to the rest of us.

The goal of top-down reform is to strengthen the structures that reinforce reciprocity, bringing more of the community of faith into the give-and-take of social power in the church. Concretely, this means the development of processes that expand dialogue, extend participation in decision-making and enlarge mutual accountability.

Expanding Dialogue

Since Vatican II there have been many efforts to expand the dialogue between the faith community and its formal leaders. Pastoral councils and priests' senates have been established at the diocesan level, school boards and parish councils now serve on the local scene. Often these groups function as advisers to those in charge rather than as bodies empowered to act. (In the American church, as Gordon Myers and Richard Schoenherr have reported, our reforms have been more successful in sharing responsibility than in sharing organizational power.) But a number of structures are now in place in dioceses and parishes and religious congregations, bringing more of the community into the conversation about its organizational life.

The process adopted by the American bishops in their preparation of the pastoral letters on peace and on the economy again points to a new openness to dialogue. Responses to early drafts of these documents were sought not only from theologians and other specialists but from the broader community as well. The dialogue among the bishops themselves was evident to the rest of us, as we became aware of the controversy and compromise that shaped each of these pastoral statements. The bishops acted here not as the unanimous and exclusive voice of Catholic morality but as prophetic leaders, setting out the transforming witness of Jesus Christ and calling their communities to the conversation about values that leads to moral decision.

Extending Decision-making

Another way in which leaders can reinforce the give-and-take of power is to broaden decision-making. By setting up working committees, by establishing procedures for discussion and debate, leaders can include more people in the choices about how the group accomplishes its tasks.

The principal at Good Shepherd Elementary School, for example, establishes a faculty curriculum committee—its job to devise ways to implement at this school the new diocesan guidelines on education for justice. The youth minister at St. Albert's Parish persuades the parish council to expand the role of the young people's coordinating committee, to give them more "say" in how the funds allocated for youth programs are used.

By broadening participation in decision-making we bring the influence of more people to bear on decisions that will affect them. The important issue here is not the *number* of decisions in which more people are involved but the *significance* of the questions that are brought to the wider group for decision. Money issues are usually bellwethers. When a group has some effective influence in budget decisions it can usually be safely assumed that this group is genuinely included in the important decisions that affect its life.

In a strategy with even wider implications, leaders can broaden participation not only in decision-making (the discussion of strategies and means) but in "authority-making" (the discussion of policy and goals). Rather than treating the group's vision and values as the province of "the few"—the pastor or the professional staff—leaders can open ways for more members to become involved in policy formulation and goal setting. The object here is to include more people in the choices about how power is to function among us. This is often a slow process, requiring considerable time in preparation.

The new pastoral staff at St. Cecilia's Church, for example, looks forward to the formation of an effective parish council, through which parishioners will have an ongoing voice in clarifying the parish's mission and evaluating its ministry goals. The recent history of the parish, however, has been somewhat autocratic. At this point there are few structures for eliciting parishioners' opinions and suggestions, and fewer yet for engaging them in any process of communal planning. This year the staff plans to establish several lay committees to assume responsibility for different areas of parish life —adult education, liturgy preparation, justice concerns. Their hope is that the parishioners who serve on these committees will gradually come into a more powerful awareness of their own participation in the life of the parish. As this awareness spreads, there will be the basis of an effective parish council. In the meantime, much of the staff's work will be devoted to spiritual formation and skill development among the parishioners.

Broadening participation in "authority-making" can also mean expanding the role that group members have in the selection of their leaders. When people are involved in the processes (whether election or appointment or merit review) that place their leaders in position, the give-and-take of power becomes more visible. This step underscores the fact that leaders work most effectively when they are accepted by the group. Usually, the more influence group members have in the selection of their leaders, the more readily the leaders gain acceptance. Leaders who come from outside—beyond the membership of the group or, more importantly, outside the group's participation—often face considerable resistance and resentment as they struggle to create an atmosphere that will allow them to function effectively.

Enlarging Accountability

Another strategy of structural purification that can be initiated from "above" is to expand the formal processes of accountability. Most institutions develop structures of vertical accountability, where leaders are accountable only to those *higher* in the organization. The local manager, for example, reports to the regional supervisor; the principal is accountable to the district superintendent; the pastor is responsible to the bishop. For the give-and-take of social power to be fully respected, leaders must "give account" to their peers and subordinates as well.

This sense of mutual accountability can be fostered in the informal setting of a peer support group, where leaders at the same level in an organization (pastors, for example, or principals or department heads) gather regularly to share information and address common concerns. As an atmosphere of trust develops, this professional support group can also become a place where colleagues can test out new ideas and comment on one another's work.

It is true that these peer groups can run the risk of isolating leaders. A priests' support group, for example, can reinforce a clerical "old boys network"; regular meetings among a group of women managers can become gripe sessions, fueling a continuing suspicion of male colleagues. The best way to avoid such insularity is to expand, not decrease, the ties that leaders have with people at many levels in the organization.

This informal network of peer accountability needs to be complemented by an effective system through which leaders can "give account" to group members as well. Gradually we are seeing these efforts take shape. An annual report from the leader on the state of the group, a series of open meetings in which the leader welcomes suggestions and responds to questions, a panel of elected representatives to serve as an advisory council for the leader—these steps support the fundamental interplay between group and leader.

This interplay becomes more robust as groups become involved in the formal evaluation of their leaders. Evaluation, whether from "top down" or from "bottom up," can be risky. Where there is insufficient trust, the formal review becomes a defensive standoff. Where there is insufficient maturity—on either part—the evaluation process becomes a pawn in a wider play for power. But when planned as part of a larger process of dialogue in the group, when carried out with competence and care, a program of performance review can be gracious—a true moment of grace, an exchange that contributes to the growth of the leader as well as to the vitality of the group. To involve members in the process of accountability reinforces an essential truth—that leaders are responsible *to* as well as *for* other members of the group.

The establishment of diocesan grievance boards and the existence of clear procedures of due process are recent developments in the church. These structures help to purify the church of one of its tyrannies: the pastor or bishop or religious superior functioning with absolute and autonomous authority in the community. The intent of these structures is to make our leaders more accountable in their exercise of power, accountable both to the faith community and to the gospel values of justice and charity.

EXERCISING THE POWERS OF THE WEAK

We have been considering here the strategies of purification that can be initiated "at the top," by persons in leadership roles. But the purification of social power does not happen simply from above. Steps taken by those in formal positions of power, as part of their responsibility for the common good, must be complemented by efforts generated from "below." Ideas emerging at the grass-roots level, initiatives taken by people in subordinate roles, demands arising among those excluded from positions of power—these are often the route of purification.

To help clarify this movement of purification from "below," we turn to the work of social analyst Elizabeth Janeway. In her book *Powers of the Weak* she examines the role of those in subordinate positions in the reform of social power.

Janeway begins with a discussion of the risks involved when reciprocity in a group is lost, when the give-and-take of social power is masked. Every group establishes a pattern of roles and relationships through which it carries on its life. While all these roles may be seen as necessary, not all will be treated as equal in value. A priority exists among these roles, with some positions—usually those of leadership—judged to be of greater value than others.

Janeway refers to those who occupy the high-status roles in a group as "the strong" and those who function in the lesser social positions as "the weak." Over time, these distinctions between the weak and the strong tend to become more pronounced. Gradually the strong gain increasing control over the resources that the group values most, whether these be wealth or wisdom or weapons.

But, Janeway reminds us, those who are socially dominant in this way do not possess their priority outright. The social privileges of those in priority roles rest on an acceptance of certain definitions of "how things are"—an acceptance not only by the privileged but by the rest of us as well.

Thus the social power of the privileged remains dependent on the attitude of the rest of us. In this sense, it is "the weak" who confer power on "the strong." They do this by accepting the current definitions of how things are and in this way granting to those in power the *right* to the privileges they claim.

Those in privileged roles are often protective of established structures. Their allegiance to the status quo is not difficult to understand, since it is "the strong" who have much to gain by leaving things as they are. Because they benefit from the current arrangement, persons in leadership positions are sometimes reluctant to undertake the difficult task of purifying the structures of power. It is the weak, who are already participants in the process of power but whose role is often concealed, whom Janeway encourages to the task.

She discusses three "powers of the weak" that equip them in this effort at structural purification. These resources enable us to recognize the limits of our current definitions of power. When the dominant definitions are questioned and the structures that flow from them are brought under review, the process of purification is begun.

The powers of the weak that Janeway discusses are the power to disbelieve; the power to come together; and the power to act in common in pursuit of shared goals.

The Power of Disbelief

The first power of the weak is disbelief. To initiate change I must disbelieve that the way things are is the way they must be, the way they *should* be. If I cannot question the status quo I am powerless to alter it.

This first power of the weak is tied to legitimacy. Legitimacy is the *right* to rule. It can be granted only by the governed. In order to be effective, those in leadership positions must be accepted by the rest of us. We need not necessarily see them as "good persons" or as "those whom we would have chosen" or even as "the best persons for the job." But if they are to be effective we must at least see them as persons whose authority is in some way justified. "I didn't vote for him; in fact I'm working actively to see that he is not reelected. But as long as he is president he has the right to be respected and obeyed." This is a statement of legitimacy.

Even in a totalitarian state legitimacy remains an important issue.

If subjects refuse to accept their leaders as legitimate, more and more of the resources of leadership must be focused on defending the right to rule and quelling social discontent. History shows that even when leaders command considerable physical force that can be used to compel acquiescence the loss of legitimacy signals the end of a regime. The experience of Ferdinand Marcos in the Philippines and the continuing turmoil in South Africa bear witness to this truth.

In granting legitimacy, followers accept the current definitions of power (what it is, who "has" it—and why) along with the structures that dictate how power is to function in the group. Most important, they accept the definition of their own position as "the weak." Those in subordinate roles begin to exercise power when they start to question these reigning definitions.

The most radical act of disbelief—going to the root of the social relationship of power—is the refusal to accept the way that those in power have defined *me*. Ultimately I come to see that the definition of myself as weak is a self-inflicted wound. I have colluded with the strong by accepting their understanding of reality. When I recognize the part I have played in my own impotence, I realize that I have options. "I have been doing this to myself; I can stop doing it." I can resist this picture of myself as powerless; I can act otherwise.

If the recognition of my collusion gives me options, it also gives me power. My social impotence is not just something that "they" are doing to me; it is something I have been doing to myself. I have been a carrier of this culture of domination. If I have been a factor in my impoverishment, I can be a factor in my empowerment. This realization—that all the power in the situation is not "theirs"—becomes an effective catalyst for change.

Disbelief stands on its own as an essential power of the weak. It is the dawn of liberation. Not until I am able to disbelieve the way that those in power have defined me will I be free to imagine alternatives to the status quo. And imagining alternatives is the first step toward their becoming possible. To disbelieve, we need not yet have an alternative to offer. We need not yet sense that others share our disbelief. These will become important if disbelief is to move us toward effective action, but disbelief alone is enough at the start.

When followers are able to question the legitimacy of their leaders they have begun to exercise the reciprocity that social structures often disguise. Social change, then, starts here. The ability to disbelieve the way the powerful have defined the situation that exists between us, the realization that their power "over" me is in part due to my acceptance of their right to rule—these changes in awareness mark a significant personal transformation. When many of us come together in this awareness we can become a potent force for social change. Consciousness-raising efforts among women and other minority-status groups in the United States, conscientization projects among the poor and politically disenfranchised in third-world countries—in these and similar ways advocates of social development attempt to nurture this first and most basic dynamic of social change. For the ordered use of power to prevail in a group setting, the ability to disbelieve must remain active among members—both those in superordinate and those in subordinate roles.

Although this first power of the weak is not illusory (Janeway and other social analysts have documented the revolutionary effects of such a change in consciousness) it is often fragile, especially in its early stages. It is here that the second power of the weak becomes crucial—the power to come together.

Coming Together

Disbelief shows us the arbitrariness of the status quo and the extent of our collusion in its negative effects. These realizations can be difficult to come to on our own; alone, they are even more difficult to sustain. It is hard to trust this new awareness when it begins to contradict what has until now seemed normal and necessary, even to me. Left alone, my growing suspicion that something is not right can begin to feel like "my problem." I may even feel crazy. My experience contradicts the prevailing wisdom; my interpretation of "what is going on here" is now at odds with the way that most other people interpret this same reality.

These statements describe what many of us experience in the early stages of social transformation. They also describe symptoms of mental illness! And it is to the advantage of "the powers that be" for this malaise to be interpreted in personal terms. As long as the causes of distress can be restricted to the private domain, as long as it is chiefly a question of psychological adjustment or even sanity, there is no cause for political alarm. And, as the provocative work of psychologist Thomas Szasz suggests, the status quo has much to gain from the "privatizing" of public distress. Resources are then focused on efforts of personal change, to help the distressed person once again to fit in, to feel comfortable with "the way things are," to accommodate to the current interpretations of what constitutes the real world. "Perhaps it is I who am troubled, not the situation." This interpretation diverts attention away from social change: underlying definitions of social power and privilege remain unquestioned; current structures remain in place.

Thus we begin to see the significance of coming together as a power of the weak. Finding others who share the new awareness helps the awareness to grow strong, even in the face of opposition. Without this experience of shared vision and shared disbelief, those in subordinate roles may feel overwhelmed by their inability to fit in. A sense of impotence and privatized pain, fostered among "the weak" by social definitions that favor "the strong," will simply be reinforced.

Since the Second Vatican Council a number of groups in the American Catholic Church have begun to disbelieve the prevailing social arrangements between the strong and the weak. These groups have begun to make public their private pain.

The Leadership Conference of Women Religious brings together the leaders of religious congregations of women in the United States. As these congregations embraced the reforms mandated by Vatican II, some found themselves at odds with ecclesiastical officials. In the midst of conflicts about the updating of their rules and constitutions, these women's groups were urged to both obedience and secrecy. Isolated from other congregations with similar questions and pains, each group found itself weak and disadvantaged. In recent years the Leadership Conference has provided a forum for sharing these stories of conflict and change. The conspiracy of secrecy broken, religious congregations are finding new strengths in shared pain and new resolve in developing a shared vision from which common action might proceed.

Another coming together in the church has occurred in the formation of support groups for gay and lesbian Catholics. Disbelieving the way they have been defined by conventional church practice, these Catholics came together to share both their faith and their distress. Their coming together has brought an area of private pain, long closeted, to public awareness. In the retreats and workshops generated by this movement, lesbian and gay Catholics are developing the outlines of a spirituality and asceticism that can practically and faithfully guide their Christian maturing.

A third group whose coming together is influencing the shape of the American church is the National Conference of Catholic Bishops. Since the council, this organization has taken on new vitality and purpose. For a long period official expectations of the bishop concentrated his ministry in his own diocese. His pastoral efforts were to be focused, even consumed, in this crucial but isolated setting. Many Vatican officials were wary of national or regional organizations of bishops, suspicious that episcopal efforts toward collegiality could only threaten the ideal of a universal uniformity.

Recent meetings, such as those held at St. John's Abbey in Minnesota, have given American bishops an opportunity to share their faith in a more profound manner. In such gatherings these leaders can also share their disbelief. Sometimes this disbelief concerns the proper role of the church in political debate in the United States; at other times it centers on the church's official stand against the ordination of women or the practice of birth control. Coming together in these ways, the American bishops are delivered from their isolation and allowed to give communal expression to their private pain and hope.

As the dialogue of faith broadens in the church, lay Catholics are startled to find that even bishops can experience themselves as impotent within church structures. They too are participants in a world of power that they cannot always influence or even fully accept. They too must find ways to come together, supporting one another both in faith and in disbelief, as they exercise their own responsibility in the purification of the structures of the church.

Shared Action

Disbelieving, we come together. In this unity we can begin to move beyond support to act for a common purpose. We are empowered by the awareness that there are many of us and that we share both hopes and needs. Our experience together helps us discern whether our cause is just. This energy can lead us to organize ourselves to do something about what we believe in common. The goal that emerges among us becomes crucial here. It must be large enough to tap the energies of our deepest hopes; it must be practical enough to offer us a real possibility of success. For Christians, the goal of our common action must be firmly rooted in the values of the gospel. Only a conviction that our own struggle contributes, in however modest a way, to the coming of the Kingdom will see us through the demanding effort of structural purification. We can trace this movement from mutual support toward common action in several places in the American church.

In 1972 Hispanic Catholics came together for the first national *Encuentro* or pastoral meeting. This gathering led to a second *Encuentro* five years later. Out of this meeting Hispanic leaders, lay and clergy, began an ambitious effort of shared action. In regional gatherings throughout the United States they solicited the feelings and hopes of other Hispanic Catholics. From a variety of sources they heard the same determination: to become contributors to the American church, not just recipients of its evangelization; to form base communities in order to share their faith with more energy; to increase the awareness of the needs of the church in Latin America. In August 1985 the fruit of this nationwide action was a third national *Encuentro,* a gathering that brought together recommendations and eleven hundred representatives from a hundred and thirty dioceses. Enlivened by these joint actions, Hispanic Catholics are planning to make a more powerful impact on the church in the United States.

A second example of concerted, common action concerns lay ministry in the American church. In 1977 a number of priests and religious, responsible for developing training programs for lay persons moving into ministry, gathered informally in Philadelphia.

They compared notes, shared information, encouraged one another and decided to meet again the following year. An annual gathering followed over the next several years, each drawing a larger number of participants into this network of mutual support. Over these years more lay persons participated in the annual meeting, reflecting an increase in the number of training programs that had lay persons as directors.

In 1981 this informal network became the National Association of Lay Ministry Coordinators. The group described itself as a professional association of priests, vowed religious and lay persons who were active in developing and administering programs of ministry training for lay people. The following years saw significant development within the association (membership continued to grow, with the largest increase among lay persons active in ministry) and beyond, as the theological and practical issues of lay ministry drew more attention in the church. In 1984 another organizational step was taken when the membership voted to change the group's name and to expand its focus. The National Association for Lay Ministry was born, its purpose to work actively at local and national levels to promote the development of lay ministry.

In these examples and others we see the power of coming together move toward the power of joint action. This movement marks a critical stage in a group's life. Many groups experience considerable strain at this stage, as they struggle with their ambition for both an inner solidarity and an outer effectiveness.

In the stage of coming together a group may have given much attention to belonging and solidarity. Now, if it is to undertake actions for social change, the group must organize itself and its resources. Agreement must be reached about tasks and roles and responsibilities. Lines of authority and accountability will need to be sketched; patterns of initiative and influence will have to be determined. Without these structures the group's efforts will lack focus and force, displaying nothing but ineffective good intentions. But the group cannot afford to let these structures of effective action develop in ways that destroy its sense of shared vision or its experience of mutual support. To be effective in social change we must remain concerned about both our life together and our success in changing the ways things are "out there." This dual concern introduces considerable tension into the group, but it is a tension that is a necessary dynamic in the maturing of any community. In our book *Community of Faith* we explore strategies that can help groups balance their commitment to both solidarity and effective action.

To better understand the dynamics of shared action, we can look to the community organization tradition in the United States. There is now a history of tested experience and analysis growing out of this effective approach to social change. In *Activism That Makes Sense,* for example, Gregory Pierce notes the importance of the transition from movement to organization. Movements are often generated by charismatic leaders. Membership in a movement is loosely defined, since people first come together around broad value commitments rather than a particular program of practical action. But, Pierce notes, "organizations, unlike movements, are after what is possible. They understand that they have limited power and that their goals and desires are often in conflict with those of other individuals and institutions which also have power."

Much of the action undertaken by movements is symbolic. Movements are given to witnessing rather than lobbying. Symbolic action is an end in itself; its goal is not so much to "accomplish" something as to draw attention to the deeper issues involved. In organizations, however, "action is a means to an end. That end is recognition by existing power centers that a new element [this organized group of people] must be considered in future decisions."

The movement in the American Catholic Church for the ordination of women seems poised at this point. For more than a decade this movement has generated conferences and sponsored symbolic action in support of its goals. Keenly aware that the characteristics of most organizations are decidedly "masculine," that is, highly structured in ways that narrow and control the flow of power, many women in the movement have resisted the transition toward greater structure. They are now struggling to create an organizational style that can combine a mutuality of power with effective social action.

Movements generate their energy by witnessing to values; it is difficult for a movement to engage in the give-and-take of practical compromise or negotiated solutions. An organization, on the other hand, has the power to negotiate. With its visible structures of leadership, its defined membership, its plan of action, an organized group can become a responsible participant in the complicated process of weighing the costs and benefits of structural transformation. "The ability to negotiate is the reason why organization is more powerful and successful than movement, and why organization will ultimately produce more real change." As a movement faces this transition into becoming an organization, it must be prepared constantly to purify the structures of power that it creates.

The purifying of power is a hardy adult endeavor. It becomes possible among us as we recognize that there are many who share the same goal. Few lay Catholics desire to seize power from the clergy in order to initiate a new tyranny. Most priests are not clinging to power as though it were their last possession. Many Catholics share the vision of a mutuality of power: a faith community differentiated by the variety of its gifts, rather than divided between those who "have power" and those who do not. Such an ambition recognizes that authority is not an abstract force magically attached to leadership but the fruit of a community's participation in power. The purification of power and authority will, in time, return religious leadership from its exile and relocate it more intimately within the community of faith.

The chief strategies of purification, we have suggested, are disbelieving and seeing through the status quo. These efforts recall the importance of prophecy among us. It is to this theme that we now turn.

REFLECTIVE EXERCISE

Consider your own experience of the powers of the weak. Recall some of the ways in which you have been involved in efforts of institutional change (for example, in the political system, in your work, in the church) or in social transformation (for example, the peace movement, the struggle for civil rights, the women's movement).

Select one of these involvements, then take some notes on it to help bring your experience to mind.

Then trace your own involvement in relation to the three powers of the weak.

- How was *disbelief* alive for you here? What part of the status quo came under question for you? What definitions of "the way things are" had to be reinterpreted or set aside?

- How did you *come together* with others? With whom did you find support? How was this solidarity nurtured and expressed?

- How was *shared action* pursued? What did this joint action achieve? What kind of organizational structure emerged? How were the tensions between solidarity and effective action resolved?

What have you learned from this effort of structural change that contributes to your future involvement in the purification of power?

ADDITIONAL RESOURCES

In *Change Agent Skills* (Brooks/Cole, 1985), Gerard Egan presents a developmental model to guide a systematic effort to purify organizational structures. Richard Sennett discusses strategies for expanding involvement in "authority making" in Part Two of *Authority* (Vintage Books, 1981). Gordon Myers and Richard Schoenherr assess the impact of new diocesan collegial structures in "The Baptism of Power," which appeared in *New Catholic World* (September/October 1980).

Elizabeth Janeway's analysis of the role of subordinates in the process of social transformation appears in *Powers of the Weak* (Knopf, 1981). Jurgen Moltmann's *The Power of the Powerless* (Crossroad Books, 1983) is a collection of sermons in which he treats biblical texts dealing with power, freedom and human liberation. In *The Strength of the Weak* (Westminster Press, 1984), Dorothee

Soelle brings together politics, feminism and liberation theology in an evocative critique of contemporary society.

Gregory F. Pierce's comments appear on p. 50 of his *Activism That Makes Sense: Congregations and Community Organization* (Paulist Press, 1984), his very readable overview of the elements of effective community organization. Charles Curran takes up the contribution of community organization to the Catholic moral tradition in "Saul D. Alinsky, Catholic Social Practice, and Catholic Theory," Chapter Seven in his *Critical Concerns in Moral Theology* (University of Notre Dame Press, 1984).

For discussion of the role of communities in processes of personal and social transformation, see our *Community of Faith: Models and Strategies for Developing Christian Communities* (Winston-Seabury, 1982), especially Chapters Five and Six.

CHAPTER TWELVE

IDOLS AND PROPHETS

The cycle of empowerment is a continuous, evolving movement. Seeing patterns of power among us leads us to preserve them in structures and institutions. These structures are the very substance of human society: they give shape to and protect our common life. But structures have a paradoxical function: they both express and restrain power. Over time, our best laws and institutions tend to become inflexible or stagnant. These "standardized" forms of power await purification. In our efforts to purify the structures that enshrine our best hopes we recognize new and long-forgotten patterns of power: the cycle begins again.

If we live today in an era especially marked by the stress of purification, it is helpful to recall that Christian history is richly patterned with such efforts. Jesus' life of recognizing patterns of God's power can also be seen as an exercise of purification. His earliest preaching ignited a reform movement *within* Jewish life. Jesus' recognition of that pattern of power that we call the Kingdom of God was really a re-recognition. He was calling his people to a purified vision of God's power. His calculated ignoring of some Sabbath laws was an exercise of purification: it invited his peers to reevaluate an overgrown system of rules and customs. The purifying of power that Jesus initiated *within* Jewish life turned out to be so radical that his followers preserved and protected it in a new and separate religious movement.

The cycle of recognizing, authorizing and purifying is also evident in the major religious movements within Christianity. Movements such as Benedict's monasticism in the sixth century and Francis of Assisi's mendicant order in the thirteenth century began as energetic efforts of recognition: each of these charismatic leaders envisioned a new pattern of religious power in Christian life. Benedict recognized the value of community life linked with a withdrawal from distraction. Following the lead of earlier efforts, he inaugurated a new style of Christian living. Francis recognized, anew, the power of a nonpossessive attitude and of harmony with creation. These recognitions captivated thousands of Christians and generated new and enduring life-styles within the Christian faith.

Subsequent generations developed rules and customs to preserve the charismatic visions of Benedict and Francis. These powerful life-styles were continuously authorized by Christians: practically by those who fruitfully lived the vocations, and officially by the church's acknowledgment of the groups as religious orders. Today these orders, along with many others, struggle in the throes of renewal: the stage of purifying power is in full swing. Renewal sends a group back to revisit the charism or originating insight of its founder. We seek to purify by re-recognizing. Effective purification combines the recovery of old visions with the unsettling energy of new visions. And the emerging blend of old recognitions and new insights must soon find expression and protection in purified structures and customs—new authorizations of Christian living.

As Catholics have become more comfortable with our own history as a continually changing vision of God's power among us, we have begun to see the Protestant Reformation in a new light. The consensus in previous generations was to view the Reformation as a departure from Catholic history, a move of infidelity, not purification. As we broaden our view of God's action beyond a more sectarian attitude, Catholics are able to include this important religious movement as *part of* Christian history. The Reformation, traumatic as it was for all its participants, begins to be recognized as part of the purifying process of Christian history. The ecumenical movement thus becomes an effort not to win the strayed back to the fold but to learn the lessons of this four-hundred-year struggle of purification, while healing the rifts in the Christian community.

IMAGES AND IDOLS

In the never ending cycle of religious maturing, two dynamics seem of especial importance. One is the inner dynamic of change itself: energetic but fragile insights survive only in organized structures and institutions. The ideal of an utterly spontaneous community, unfettered by rules and roles, is a romantic fantasy. Our best hopes, generated in sudden vision or charismatic insight, only endure by being protected in social structures. The second dynamic is that by which communities slip into stagnation. This experience of institutional demise merits some special attention.

In our efforts to protect the community's deepest values we build structures—organizations, laws, liturgies—that will both hold and preserve them. To protect our values against the abuses of misinterpretation and malpractice we encase them in doctrine and rules of action; we enshrine them. A conviction of Jesus is wrapped in a story, then distilled in an official dogma. Gradually this protective sanctuary comes to represent the original experiences (of presence or conversion or forgiveness) and even to replace them. Designed to safeguard and "showcase" our deepest values, doctrine and dogma can tend gradually to replace the need for a direct experience. The ritual of devotional confession, repeated again and again, can come to replace a change of heart; a liturgy, repeated daily and privately, can seem to guarantee grace without the need for a more visceral experience of community.

This is an ordinary dynamic of human change: institutions first protect and then replace values; laws first safeguard and then replace religious experience. The clarity of the catechism substitutes for the confusing parable of Jesus' life. Metaphors of religious power, such as conversion, Eucharist, or a creed, are enshrined and gradually become idols. Theologian David Power, in his *Gifts That Differ*, describes this inevitable process as one of "sedimentation":

> Sedimentation of a symbol occurs when the symbol is translated into a conceptual meaning or is made to support a definite juridical structure, and such a meaning is then the only one attached to the symbol (p. 117).

This sedimentation reduces the plural, suggestive meanings of a symbol or metaphor to a single, institutionally sanctioned meaning. The threat to the metaphor's continued gracefulness is recognized in the next step of the process that David Power describes: the image now "does not evoke new inquiry or reflection." Its loss of liveliness and its servitude to institutional purposes signal that the image is becoming an idol.

This is, admittedly, a somewhat different theology of idolatry. In ancient Israel idols were images of *others'* gods. The golden calf was an image of a false god worshiped by aliens. But there is another peril *within* the believing community: there are domestic idols. These are images of God's power that have grown rigid and ungraceful. Not portraits of false gods or others' gods, these are once holy images that, without our noticing it, have lost their gracefulness. The practices of devotional confession, the private Mass, the recitation of creeds are not *false* images; they are not from the start ill conceived. But when the religious experiences of forgiveness, celebration and believing are encased too rigidly in ritual or catechetical repetition their enshrinement becomes an entombment. Metaphors are made into idols. This may be the case with hierarchy as an image of our shared life: though it once served as a useful self-portrait, it no longer gracefully reveals us to ourselves. It encases us in a social arrangement that restricts the flow of charism and service. For us to cling to this metaphor and to resist its purification is to make of this image a domestic idol.

This theology of idols is rooted in a double conviction: we experience God through images and symbols; yet we are to avoid "graven images" (Exodus 20:4). How are we to rely on images of God's presence in our lives while preventing them from becoming "graven"? From our religious beginnings, images of God's power have been necessary and unavoidable. The burning bush, the tent of visitation, manna, the Torah as the book of God's law—all of these stand as early and enduring metaphors of God's presence in human life. These images give a definite shape and specific focus to the ubiquitous power of God. Jesus' experience of baptism, of his final supper and of the cross became symbols of God's special presence in his life and ours—conversion, communal celebration, life from death.

For Jews and Christians, and for all religious believers, the question arises: how to prevent these compelling images from becoming graven? A graven image is one that becomes both inscribed and entrenched in our life; such an image provides not only an outline or sketch of God's presence but an *engraved* portrait. The figure becomes too defined and inflexible. Rigid and self-important, it soon distracts us from the very power it represents. Gradually the image replaces God's power; the symbol substitutes for religious experience; the metaphor replaces faith. Graven and self-serious, the once graceful image has become an idol.

Icons and Idols

Theologian Jaroslav Pelikan provides a brief and clear statement of this danger of idolatry. Addressing Christians' relation to their own past (Scripture and our two-thousand-year tradition), Pelikan distinguishes three ways of viewing our religious heritage. Our Scriptures and history serve us most adequately as *icons:* an icon "bids us look at it, but through it, and beyond it, to that living reality of which it is an embodiment." The Scriptures and church institutions are meant to embody God's presence in the world; they stand as icons, giving God's grace a tangible shape.

But a religious past, with its texts and laws and organizations, can also function as a *token:* here the Christian tradition becomes "a purely arbitrary representation that does not embody what it represents." Thus a bureaucratic church, absorbed in political infighting, becomes unbelievable. Meeting it, we may give it "token respect," but we cannot see in it the grace of God.

Thirdly, a religious tradition can become an *idol:* worse than a token, our past becomes an end in itself. Texts and institutions are adhered to in the false hope that *they* will save us. Orthodoxy itself seems to guarantee our salvation. Here the images that comprise the tradition become graven images, golden calves, replacing the Holy One they are meant to reveal.

Icon, token, idol: how do these different uses of religious imagery fit our exploration of religious leadership? Leaders and institutions of leadership (such as priesthood) are meant to act as icons —transparent images through which we experience God's leadership. A graceful leader does not absorb our devotion but allows us to touch God. This is what we mean when we say that a Christian leader is a representative of God. But images of leadership, if untended and unpurified, gradually become tokens.

"Token" suggests irrelevance: not a graven image, this is a metaphor that no longer "works." It no longer evokes among us—easily and authentically—a glimpse of God's presence and care. An example here is the metaphor of the leader as shepherd. This image of care and guidance carried considerable weight in the pastoral societies of our religious past. In a predominantly urban world this once graceful image gradually becomes a token: invoked repeatedly in our liturgies, it embodies for fewer and fewer Christians a compelling vision of human and divine leadership. A contemporary urban community, alive with very different images, is likely to hear in this metaphor not its pastoral warmth but the previously ignored implication about the group: a witless flock of sheep waiting for its leader.

Metaphors of leadership, meant to be icons, can also become idols. Here an image of leadership or its official structure becomes an obstacle to recognizing God's presence and guidance. The image takes center stage, attracts attention to itself, demands compliance. Instead of pointing to God as an icon, it substitutes for the Holy, becoming an idol. For more and more Catholics "hierarchy" as an image of the church is becoming such a metaphor. This portrait of a vertical world separated into different levels (regal and priestly leaders above; lay Christians below) was borrowed from the early church's cultural milieu. As the church grew, this metaphor became more and more enshrined in legal statutes and institutions. Church leaders came to argue that this metaphor of community structure was, in fact, God's eternal will for the church. Defended as a nonnegotiable portrait of Christian life, "hierarchy" gradually becomes a graven image. When this structure obstructs the purifying of Christian ministry, it distracts our vision instead of leading us to see God.

This degenerative process reminds us of the nature of metaphors: they are suggestive and elusive, overflowing with meaning. Spun out by our imaginations, they give us hints and clues about the movement of God's power among us. But these images are also, as human artifacts, limited; they have a shadow side. The process of authorizing patterns of power among us necessarily involves the selection and emphasis of certain metaphors of community and leadership. The dynamic of stagnation sets in as these images begin to be taken literally: "priest" becomes not merely a suggestive way to picture the community leader (as it was in second and third centuries) but the exclusive and literal definition of the leader. The metaphor becomes inflexible and political as it is used to argue for the restriction of sacramental leadership to men. The ancient and compelling image of "priest," institutionally enshrined, gradually becomes an idol. Employed to legislate a highly restrictive view of community leadership, it blocks our vision of God rather than mediating it.

In a period of stagnation and idolatry catechisms and textbooks flourish. A concise and unambiguous outline of the faith first assists and then replaces the more complex exercise of adult belief. The more bewildering aspects of faith—the rough edges, odd tastes and dark corners of religious living—are edited out or "standardized" for general consumption. But shrines and idols, however orthodox, cannot contain the movement of God's power, and purification begins again.

Religious faith, as exercised throughout this cycle of empowerment, leads us from imagination (recognizing power) to enshrinement (authorizing power) to iconoclasm (purifying power). We cannot do without images of who God is, of how leaders act, of how the community is structured. But we can barely do with them. Purifying patterns of power necessitates an exercise of iconoclasm: we break the metaphors and images of our faith that have grown rigid and inflexible. Purification also involves us in grieving, for these images—of the Eucharist as a sacrifice, of the church as a hierarchy, of sacramental leaders as necessarily male—are deep in our bones. As a religious tradition, we depart from them only with some mourning and painful leave-taking.

Communities of faith and religious traditions that cannot break their domestic idols slip further and further into stagnation. A group may cling to ancient but petrified images of faith, fearful that if they break their idols they will be punished. Or they may fear that if they clear out this shrine there will be nothing to replace it.

Paralyzed, a group may continue to cling to metaphors even when they no longer quicken faith. Patterns of power, now frozen in rigid idols, become magical and coercive. The stage of purifying patterns of power invites us to leave our shrines and idols in pursuit of a moving God. We hear again the warning of Yahweh, spoken by the prophet Nathan against building too grand a temple: "I have never stayed in a house from the day I brought the Israelites out of Egypt until today, but have always led a wanderer's life in a tent" (II Samuel 7:6).

Different Styles of Leadership

In the post-Vatican II period of purifying patterns of power, we are recognizing the great array of leadership styles that are needed in the church. As we reexamine the life of Jesus Christ portrayed in the gospels, we see a style that is most emphatically one of seeing and announcing. This kerygmatic style of leading is essential to Jesus' role in initiating a new way of religious living. The Christian ministries of preaching and witness as ancillary styles of leadership flow from Jesus' role as an announcer.

In the centuries of Christian faith during which Jesus' vision was being authorized in various organizations and doctrines, the *protector* style of leadership emerged and began to dominate. Leaders during a time of authorizing tend to be managers and judges. Organizational growth and law require specific styles of leadership: the bishop who had been a local pastor in the second century becomes a regional administrator in the fifth century. The normal tendency of such a period is for leadership to be authorized in the predominant mode of management. Since these regional administrators were also law makers, ruling and judging receive increased emphasis. During these centuries Jesus leadership style came, in fact, to be imaged as one of ruling and judging. Thus Christians began to celebrate Christ as king and judge. The ministry of priests and bishops, as representatives of Christ, was increasingly portrayed as that of ruler and judge.

We see here again the inherent danger of the process of authorizing: images and metaphors that are originally suggestive become, in time, prescriptive: *one* style of leading tends to dominate and even eliminate other styles. In Christian history the image of the leader-king and leader-judge increasingly replaced Jesus' historical leadership styles of teaching and prophecy. The celebration of Christ as Lord *(Dominus)* replaces that of Christ as teacher and prophet. And this lordship or dominion of Christ is transferred, vicariously, to the leaders of Christian communities. Dominion or lordship may fit Christ's leadership but only with great danger is it applied to the service of his followers. The danger lies in the kinship of dominion with domination. Too easily, lordship slips into "lording it over" in the way that Jesus warned us against (Mark 10:42–43); dominion is only a step from domination. When a variety of leadership styles are reduced to a single style such as lordship, the metaphor of dominion begins to slip toward the religious idol of domination.

In a period of purification we experience the call to break the idol of domination as a style of Christian leadership and to reimagine new styles of service to one another. Such reimagining is, of course, a remembering of other ancient images of leadership: after a long moratorium, prophets begin to appear in the land. Leaders with powerful imaginations invite us to see alternatives to "the way things are." They call us to recognize the customs and habits that are dying. They encourage us to let go, even when we are not sure about what comes next.

This never ending cycle alerts us that the church needs different styles of leadership at various times in its life. But it also teaches us about the pluralism of leadership in general. To cling exclusively to one style of leadership, baptizing it as "Jesus' leadership" or God's will, is to invite stagnation and idolatry. Communities of faith are complex and changing realities, with many and shifting needs. A vital faith will respond with images of the many different styles of leadership that communities need for their religious life to flourish. This faith will also embolden us to let go rigid and dominating styles of leadership and try other, more graceful styles of service.

PURIFYING POWER—A PROPHETIC PROCESS

We have been suggesting that the process of purifying patterns of power is an ordinary part of our religious heritage. A church that describes itself as "always to be reformed" must expect both to authorize patterns of power in Scripture and ministry and continually to purify these authorizations. This process, while crucial to our communal maturing, poses considerable threat: it brings authority under constant scrutiny, subjecting it to criticism and change. For this reason the process of purifying power has, more than once, been "forgotten" in Christian history. Because of its revolutionary implications this process bears further analysis. A process of purifying power is, in fact, an exercise of Christian prophecy. It performs the three functions of ancient prophecy: seeing through, disbelieving and mourning.

Seeing Through

Prophecy, whether in ancient Israel or in contemporary America, begins in vision. The popular myth about prophets was that they see details of life in the distant future. More accurately, prophets are persons blessed by a more immediate and practical vision. The prophet, as Scripture scholar Walter Brueggemann has so well illuminated in his *The Prophetic Imagination,* is able to see through the present. Just before the fall of Jerusalem in 587 the prophet Jeremiah saw his community's sinfulness. He saw through the complacency of the present situation and warned the nation's leaders of an imminent downfall. Most of the people of Jerusalem "could not see" his point and dismissed his speeches as rantings of a disturbed person. So Jerusalem fell and the Israelites were led, in shame, into exile in a foreign land.

The vision of the prophet discerns a movement in contemporary life; it is a recognition, however faint or hesitant, of God's invitation to a group to continue their journey, leaving behind some part of their former life. The barrier to such vision is the present itself: the distractions, delights and comforts of this locale divert our attention from God's call. The present has become thoroughly "authorized"—well established, legitimate, defended. The present is always, in some sense, the orthodox. It tends to express and protect, in Brueggemann's foreboding phrasing, "the royal consciousness."

The prophetic person or group is given the gift to see through this status quo which, in its stability, wraps us in a religious amnesia about journeys, leave-takings and other purifications. Little wonder that the prophet is so rarely a well-regarded figure. In Vatican II a sufficient number of prophets—lay, vowed religious and clergy—saw through the present and urged the church to a long and arduous process of purification. This prophetic process seems to have just begun.

Disbelieving

To see through the present we must learn to disbelieve it. Prophecy, begun in vision, leads to the perilous virtue of disbelief. Disbelief, as we saw in Chapter Eleven, is essential to the process of transformation. When we begin to see through the way things are (likely pictured as "the way we have always done it"), we gain another, often more threatening perspective. We see alternatives to the present and begin to question some of the images that had defined us. Since the 1960s lay Catholics have become increasingly uncomfortable with a piety that portrays them as passive and docile children. Women have begun to refuse the authorized view of them as unacceptable candidates for priestly leadership. We have started to doubt the traditional view that Protestants are heretics (or worse). Prophetic vision has generated disbelief. It has found practical expression in a new kind of disobedience. This disobedience is not a turn away from God; it is a challenge to the patterns of power that had become authorized over recent centuries in Catholic life.

As biblical scholarship and historical research provided alternate images of liturgy and ministry and the sacraments we began to "see through" our most recent past. The most significant belief shattered in this painful movement of purification was the vision of our religious world itself. We began to see through the wonderfully simple but no longer persuasive vision of that world as stable and sure, insured by a single unerring authority. As we started to disbelieve this officially authorized self-portrait, we were beset by feelings ranging from guilt to euphoria. This new and unnerving disbelief was supported by an alternate vision of the world and by evocative models of disobedience.

The new vision was of a religious world of plural authorities. Suddenly (it seemed) we found ourselves among a variety of authoritative voices: Scripture, personal conscience, a community's discernment, our shared history of two thousand years, canon law, the magisterium. Within the Scriptures themselves plural authorities appeared: voices in the New Testament conflicted with demands heard in the Hebrew Scriptures; the four gospels were recognized as more authoritative than the later pastoral epistles. An unsettling responsibility descended on the Catholic individual and community: no longer children who had only to obey, we were called to an adult participation in the continuing authorizing of our Christian faith.

The models that instructed those of us who were new at the virtue of disobedience came to us from abroad as well as from closer at hand. In India, Gandhi had demonstrated a holy disobedience that challenged the structures of British colonialism. In our own country, Martin Luther King was disobeying state laws that authorized a segregated vision of American society. Both of these extraordinary persons exercised disobedience *as a virtue*—a carefully disciplined action in the pursuit of a religious ideal. These two, joined by such prophets as the Berrigans and other protesters against the Vietnam War, compelled Catholics to new visions and unlikely virtues.

Mourning

Prophecy, and the purification it engenders, begins in vision and disbelief. Both of these exercises lead to grief. When we embrace a new vision of life together we necessarily take leave of an old vision; when we disbelieve we enter a process of grieving.

Christians, especially those with Anglo-Saxon roots, have not cherished grieving. And yet it is, or can become, a Christian virtue. Grieving is the ability to mourn, to both let go and retain past parts of ourselves. Grieving, as a necessary confrontation with loss and change, has been carefully studied by researchers such as Elizabeth Kübler-Ross, Colin Murray Parkes and Peter Marris. The complex passage of mourning, often lasting for several years, leads us through stages of denial, anger and blame, letting go and resolution.

Subsequent research, undertaken by J. Gordon Myers at the University of Wisconsin in Madison, has charted the maturing of small groups in relation to their ability to grieve. Only as the group lets go former assumptions—for example, about who is in charge or how close members should become in the group—can it develop toward a new stage of maturity. Myers' research suggests that a "focal person" (someone in whom the group's distress has a special resonance) often plays a prophetic role in the group's maturing. Walter Brueggemann's analysis of ancient prophecy reinforces this connection between grieving and group maturity. The prophet, whether Jeremiah or Gandhi or Martin Luther King, calls us to mourn a way of life that is dying. As Gordon Myers has described it, the "focal person" as prophet invites us to a funeral we do not want to attend.

In the 1960s the Catholic Church came alive with a new enthusiasm generated by the Vatican Council. In this honeymoon period we rejoiced in a revitalized liturgy, a hope of shared leadership and a recovery of our social conscience. Two decades later, as we move into a post-romantic phase of church renewal, we realize we have yet to mourn fully the changes taking place in our religious life. The world we left in the 1960s (or, at least, began to be coaxed from) had its charm: the priest knew what was best for the parish; the Sisters and Brothers instructed our children in the faith; our roles and rules were clear. It was an idyllic, if childish, world for many Catholics. Even as we rejoiced in the changes of Vatican II, we still carried old structures and expectations deep in our hearts. And we were taking leave of this world at quite different speeds. In our corporate grieving some of us lingered at the stage of anger and blame, finding it very difficult to let go such a cherished way of life. A few of us remained at the even earlier stage of denial: this is not happening.

Very many struggled through the letting go while wondering if all this change meant that the "old way" was all wrong. Is our past suddenly to be rejected? Does embracing the new demand a repudiation of who we have been? Indeed, in a dualistic vision of the world, with its dichotomies of good and bad, we can let go only of the bad. We are faced with simple but harsh choices. But in a more complex world of many goods, we learn to let go parts of our past —not because they are evil or shameful but because they do not fit the future. Past forms of the liturgy or styles of ministry are not to

be set aside because they are foolish or sinful. In fact these have
served us well in many ways. But they do not fit the future into
which God is leading us. We journey toward new forms of ministry
and liturgy only as we grieve for old ones, as we mourn and let go
what were once graceful ways of being together.

In any passage of grieving we are asked to let go of some accustomed or cherished parts of ourselves. Something very important to
us is dying. A threatening question intrudes: Will we survive? Will
we still be Catholics, after all these changes? It helps to remember
that this question has been asked before. The Israelites wondered
if, deprived of their temple and led into exile, they would still be
the people of God. The first generation of Christians asked if they
could abandon the practice of circumcision and still be followers of
Jesus. Only gradually, through resistance and regret, are we able to
let go. We die to a way of life and slowly forge a renewed life. This
is precisely what the Catholic Church is doing today. As we purify
the patterns of power and authority and leadership, we mourn. As
our former world is turned upside down, we feel some of the stress
that Paul recognized in his own time. With him, we testify that "All
creation is groaning. . . ." All the church is groaning as we let go
old styles of leadership and accustomed forms of worship and ministry. The groaning is painful, but it is a sign of life. The body Christian is not dying but stirring. It is moving in new and unfamiliar
ways. The groaning is prophetic: mourning what must die, we respond to God's invitation to purify the patterns of power that structure our life of faith. We move into an unknown future, confident
that it is our God who leads us on this journey.

REFLECTIVE EXERCISE

To better appreciate the dynamics of institutional grieving in the
church today, reflect on the place of mourning in your own life.

Return to a significant experience of personal grief—the death of
a loved one, the loss of a valued ideal, a profound personal failure.
Be gentle with yourself as these memories come, perhaps bringing
with them some pain and confusion.

Can you recall the dominant emotions of that time, your struggle with denial or resistance or anger? What helped you face the loss and accept the discipline of letting go? How does this loss survive in you still—as a wound or as a regret or as a gift?

Are there places in the life of the church these days where you recognize a similar process of grief? Concretely, what is the shape of the death or loss that threatens? Which of the emotions of grief —denial, anger, blame, guilt—are most in evidence? How can this community of faith be helped to name its sorrow and move toward its future in hope?

From your awareness of the dynamics of personal grief, what do you learn about an effective ministry to the church in a time of loss and renewal.

ADDITIONAL RESOURCES

David Power's discussion of the "sedimentation" of symbols is in his study of lay ministry, *Gifts That Differ* (Pueblo, 1980), p. 117. Also see his more recent *Unsearchable Riches: The Symbolic Nature of Liturgy* (Pueblo, 1984). Jaroslav Pelikan's reflection on icons and idols appears in *The Vindication of Tradition* (Yale University Press, 1984).

There is a rich fund of scholarship devoted to the religious imagination and the journey of the religious metaphor from fantasy, through idolatry, toward a faithful vision of reality. See William Lynch's *Images of Hope* (University of Notre Dame Press, 1974) and *Images of Faith* (University of Notre Dame Press, 1973); Paul Ricoeur's *The Symbolism of Evil* (Beacon Press, 1967) and *Freud and Philosophy* (Yale University Press, 1970). Maria Harris explores imagination as a theological and pastoral resource in *Teaching and Religious Imagination* (Harper & Row, 1986).

Walter Brueggemann explores contemporary ministry in the light of ancient prophecy in his excellent book *The Prophetic Imagination* (Fortress Press, 1978). Of special interest are his linking of the prophetic challenges of vision and criticism, insight and grieving.

J. Gordon Myers' research on the role of grieving in the process of group maturing is reported in *Grief Work as a Critical Condition for Small Group Phase Development*, available through the Laboratory for the Study of Small Groups at the University of Wisconsin/Madison. Elizabeth Kübler-Ross is a pioneer in the study of the personal experience of grief; see her *Death: The Final Stage of Growth* (Prentice-Hall, 1975). In *Bereavement: Studies of Grief in Adult Life* (Tavistock, 1972) Colin Murray Parkes reports the findings of systematic research on the grieving process. Peter Marris broadens the discussion on grief to include social phenomena as well as personal loss; see his *Loss and Change* (Doubleday, 1975).

Prophetic voices in many quarters call the American Catholic community to the tasks of purification. For more than two decades theologian Rosemary Ruether has provided careful and critical analysis of the structures of Christian faith. See, for example, her *The Radical Kingdom* (Paulist Press, 1975) and *New Woman, New Earth: Sexist Ideologies and Human Liberation* (Seabury Press, 1975). In his pastoral letter on ministry, *In Service of One Another,* Joseph Cardinal Bernardin calls the faithful to recognize that ministry is rooted in the sacraments of initiation and to repudiate the "ranking" of the diverse ministries in the community of faith. William J. Bausch stresses the importance of the needs and experience of the faith community itself in determining the shape of its future structures in *Ministry: Traditions, Tensions, Transitions* (Twenty-third Publications, 1983).

BIBLIOGRAPHY

Abbott, Walter M., ed. *The Documents of Vatican II.* New York: America Press, 1966.

Anderson, Bernard. *Understanding the Old Testament.* 3rd Edition. Englewood Cliffs, N.J.: Prentice-Hall, 1975.

Bailey, F. G. *The Tactical Uses of Passion.* Ithaca, N.Y.: Cornell University Press, 1983.

Bausch, William J. *Ministry: Traditions, Tensions, Transitions.* Mystic, Conn.: Twenty-Third Publications, 1983.

Bennis, Warren, and Burt Nanus. *Leaders.* New York: Harper & Row, 1985.

Bernardin, Joseph Cardinal. "In Service of One Another," *Origins* (August 1985), pp. 132–38.

Boff, Leonard. *Church: Charism and Power.* New York: Crossroad Books, 1985.

Brewer, James H., J. Michael Ainsworth and George E. Wynne. *Power Management.* Englewood Cliffs, N.J.: Prentice-Hall, 1984.

Brown, Raymond. *The Community of the Beloved Disciple.* New York: Paulist Press, 1979.

Brueggemann, Walter. *The Prophetic Imagination.* Philadelphia: Fortress Press, 1978.

Burns, James McGregor. *Leadership.* New York: Harper & Row, 1978.

Christian Brothers Conference. *Power and Authority.* Lockport, Ill.: Christian Brothers' National Office, 1976.

Congar, Yves. "The Historical Development of Authority in the Church: Points for Christian Reflection," pp. 119–53. In John M. Todd, ed., *Problems of Authority.* Baltimore: Helicon, 1962.

Cooke, Bernard. *Sacraments and Sacramentality.* Mystic, Conn.: Twenty-Third Publications, 1983.

Curran, Charles. "Saul D. Alinsky, Catholic Social Practice, and

Catholic Theory," in his *Critical Concerns in Moral Theology*. Notre Dame, Ind.: University of Notre Dame Press, 1984.

Dodd, E. R. *The Greeks and the Irrational*. Los Angeles: University of California Press, 1951.

Doohan, Helen. *Leadership in Paul*. Wilmington, Del.: Michael Glazier, 1984.

Dozier, Verna J. *The Authority of the Laity*. Washington, D.C.: Alban Institute, 1980.

Dulles, Avery. "Institution and Charism in the Church," pp. 18–40 in his *A Church to Believe In*. New York: Crossroad Books, 1982.

————. *Models of the Church*. Garden City, N.Y.: Doubleday, 1974.

Egan, Gerard. *Change Agent Skills*. Monterey, Cal.: Brooks/Cole, 1985.

Eisenstein, Hester, and Alice Jardine, eds. *The Future of Difference*. New Brunswick, N.J.: Rutgers University Press, 1985.

Emerson, Richard. "Power-Dependence Relations," *American Sociological Review* (February 1962), pp. 30–38.

Erikson, Erik. *Insight and Responsibility*. New York: Norton, 1964.

Fenhagen, James C. *Mutual Ministry: New Vitality for the Local Church*. Minneapolis: Winston-Seabury Press, 1977.

Fiorenza, Elizabeth Schüssler. *In Memory of Her*. New York: Crossroad Books, 1983.

Gamble, Harry. *The New Testament Canon*. Philadelphia: Fortress Press, 1985.

Gibb, Cecil A., ed. *Leadership: Selected Readings*. Baltimore: Penguin, 1969.

Gilmour, Peter. *The Emerging Parish*. Kansas City: Sheed & Ward, 1986.

Greeley, Andrew. *American Catholics Since the Council*. Chicago: Thomas More Press, 1985.

Greenleaf, Robert K. *Servant Leadership*. New York: Paulist Press, 1977.

Guzie, Tad. *The Book of Sacramental Basics*. New York: Paulist Press, 1981.

————. *Jesus and the Eucharist*. New York: Paulist Press, 1974.

Hagberg, Janet O. *Real Power: Stages of Personal Power in Organizations*. Minneapolis: Winston Press, 1984.

Hahn, Cecilia A., and James R. Adams. *The Mystery of Clergy Authority*. Washington, D.C.: Alban Institute, 1979.

Harris, John C. *Stress, Power and Ministry.* Washington, D.C.: Alban Institute, 1977.

Harris, Maria. *Teaching and Religious Imagination.* San Francisco: Harper & Row, 1986.

Hengel, Martin. *Christ and Power.* Philadelphia: Fortress Press, 1977.

Holmberg, Bengt. *Paul and Power.* Philadelphia: Fortress Press, 1978.

Janeway, Elizabeth. *Powers of the Weak.* New York: Knopf, 1981.

Jaubert, Annie. "Les Épîtres de Paul: le fait communautaire," pp. 16–33. In Jean Delorme, ed., *Le Ministère et les ministères selon le Nouveau Testament.* Paris: Éditions de Seuil, 1974.

Kaesemann, Ernst. *Perspectives on Paul.* London: SCM Press, 1971.

Kanter, Rosabeth Moss. *Men and Women of the Corporation.* New York: Basic Books, 1976.

Kegan, Robert. *The Evolving Self: Problem and Process in Human Development.* Cambridge: Harvard University Press, 1982.

Kennedy, Eugene. *The Now and Future Church: The Psychology of Being an American Catholic.* Garden City, N.Y.: Doubleday, 1984.

Kinast, Robert. *Caring for Society: A Theological Interpretation of Lay Ministry.* Chicago: Thomas More Press, 1985.

Kübler-Ross, Elizabeth. *Death: The Final Stage of Growth.* Englewood Cliffs, N.J.: Prentice-Hall, 1975.

Lassey, William R., and Marshall Sashkin, eds. *Leadership and Social Change.* Rev. 3rd ed. San Diego, Cal.: University Associates, 1983.

Léon-Dufour, Xavier. *Dictionary of Biblical Theology.* New York: Crossroad Books, 1977.

Lips, Hilary M. *Women, Men, and the Psychology of Power.* Englewood Cliffs, N.J.: Prentice-Hall, 1981.

Loomer, Bernard. "Two Kinds of Power," *Criterion: Journal of the University of Chicago Divinity School* (Winter, 1976), pp. 11–29.

Lynch, William. *Images of Faith.* Notre Dame, Ind.: University of Notre Dame Press, 1973.

————. *Images of Hope.* Notre Dame, Ind.: University of Notre Dame Press, 1974.

Malcolm, Janet. *Psychoanalysis: The Impossible Profession.* New York: Vintage Books, 1981.

Marris, Peter. *Loss and Change.* Garden City, N.Y.: Doubleday, 1975.

Martos, Joseph. *Doors to the Sacred.* Garden City, N.Y.: Doubleday, 1981.

May, Rollo. *Love and Will.* New York: Delta, 1969.

McCormick, Richard. *Notes on Moral Theology, 1965 through 1980.* Lanham, Md.: University Press of America, 1981.

McKenzie, John L. *Authority in the Church.* Kansas City: Sheed & Ward, 1966; 1986.

Mitchell, Nathan. *Mission and Ministry.* Wilmington, Del.: Michael Glazier, 1982.

Mohler, James. *The Origin and Evolution of the Priesthood.* New York: Alba House, 1970.

Moltmann, Jurgen. *The Power of the Powerless.* New York: Crossroad Books, 1983.

Murray, John Courteney. *We Hold These Truths: Catholic Reflections on the American Proposition.* Kansas City: Sheed & Ward, 1960; 1986.

Myers, J. Gordon. *Grief Work as a Critical Condition for Small Group Phase Development.* 1986. Available through the Laboratory for the Study of Small Groups at the University of Wisconsin in Madison, Wisconsin.

Myers, J. Gordon, and John J. Lawyer. *A Guidebook for Problem Solving in Group Settings.* Kansas City, Mo.: Sheed & Ward, 1985.

Myers, J. Gordon, and Richard Schoenherr. "The Baptism of Power," *New Catholic World* (September/October 1980), pp. 217–20.

Newman, John Cardinal. *On Consulting the Faithful in Matters of Doctrine.* Kansas City: Sheed & Ward, 1961; 1986.

Nisbet, Robert A. "Authority," pp. 107–73 in his *The Sociological Tradition.* New York: Basic Books, 1967.

O'Meara, Thomas. *Theology of Ministry.* New York: Paulist Press, 1983.

Osiek, Carolyn. "Relation of Charism to Rights and Duties in the New Testament Church," pp. 41–59. In James Provost, ed., *Official Ministry in a New Age.* Washington, D.C.: Canon Law Society of America, 1981.

Oswald, Roy. *Power Analysis of a Congregation.* Washington, D.C.: Alban Institute, 1982.

Parkes, Colin Murray. *Bereavement: Studies of Grief in Adult Life.* London: Tavistock, 1972.

Pelikan, Jaroslav. *The Vindication of Tradition.* New Haven, Conn.: Yale University Press, 1984.

Pierce, Gregory F. *Activism That Makes Sense: Congregations and Community Organization.* New York: Paulist Press, 1984.

Powell, Cyril. *The Biblical Concept of Power.* New York: Epworth, 1963.

Power, David. "The Basis for Official Ministry in the Church," pp. 60–88. In James Provost, ed., *Official Ministry in a New Age.* Washington, D.C.: Canon Law Society of America, 1981.

––––––. *Gifts That Differ: Lay Ministries Established and Unestablished.* New York: Pueblo, 1980.

––––––. "Liturgy and Empowerment." In Michael Cowan, ed., *Alternate Futures of Worship: Christian Leadership.* Collegeville, Minn.: Liturgical Press, 1987.

––––––. *Unsearchable Riches: The Symbolic Nature of Liturgy.* New York: Pueblo, 1984.

Rahner, Karl. *Theological Investigations, XIX.* New York: Crossroad Books, 1983.

Reed, Bruce. *The Dynamics of Religion.* London: Darton, Longman & Todd, 1978.

Ricoeur, Paul. *Freud and Philosophy.* New Haven, Conn.: Yale University Press, 1970.

––––––. *The Symbolism of Evil.* Boston: Beacon Press, 1967.

Ruether, Rosemary. *New Woman, New Earth: Sexist Ideologies and Human Liberation.* New York: Seabury Press, 1975.

––––––. *The Radical Kingdom.* New York: Paulist Press, 1975.

Russell, Letty. *The Future of Partnership.* Philadelphia: Westminster Press, 1979.

––––––. *Growth in Partnership.* Philadelphia: Westminster Press, 1981.

Schein, Edgar H. *Organizational Culture and Leadership.* San Francisco: Jossey-Bass, 1985.

Schillebeeckx, Edward. *The Church with a Human Face.* New York: Crossroad Books, 1985.

––––––. *Jesus: An Experiment in Christology.* New York: Random House, 1981.

––––––. *Ministry: Leadership in the Community of Jesus Christ.* New York: Crossroad Books, 1981.

Schoenherr, Richard. "Power and Authority in Organized Religion," *Sociological Analysis,* in press.

Schütz, John Howard. *Paul and Apostolic Authority.* Cambridge: Cambridge University Press, 1975.

Sennett, Richard. *Authority.* New York: Vintage Books, 1981.

Soelle, Dorothee. *The Strength of the Weak.* Philadelphia: Westminster Press, 1984.

Stendahl, Krister. "The Bible as Classic and the Bible as Holy Scripture," *Journal of Biblical Literature,* 103 (1984).

Swain, Bernard. *Liberating Leadership: Practical Styles for Pastoral Ministry.* Minneapolis: Winston Press, 1986.

Sweetser, Thomas, and Carol Wisniewski Holden. *Leadership in a Successful Parish.* San Francisco: Harper & Row, 1986.

Swidler, Leonard. "Demo-Kratia, The Rule of the People of God, or Consensus Fidelium," pp. 226–43. In Leonard Swidler and Piet Fransen, eds., *Authority in the Church and the Schillebeeckx Case.* New York: Crossroad Books, 1982.

Thompson, William G. *The Gospels for Your Whole Life: Mark and John in Prayer and Study.* Minneapolis: Winston-Seabury, 1984.

———. *Paul and His Message for Life's Journey.* New York: Paulist Press, 1986.

Tracy, David. *The Analogical Imagination.* New York: Crossroad Books, 1981.

Ulrich, Eugene C., and William G. Thompson. "The Tradition as a Resource in Theological Reflection—Scripture and the Minister," pp. 31–52. In James D. Whitehead and Evelyn Eaton Whitehead, *Method in Ministry: Theological Reflection and Christian Ministry.* Minneapolis: Winston-Seabury, 1981.

Whitehead, Evelyn Eaton, and James D. Whitehead. *Community of Faith: Models and Strategies for Developing Christian Communities.* Minneapolis: Winston-Seabury, 1982.

Whitehead, James. "Stewardship: The Disciple Becomes a Leader." In Michael Cowan, ed., *Alternate Futures of Worship: Christian Leadership.* Collegeville, Minn.: Liturgical Press, 1987.

Whitehead, James D., and Evelyn Eaton Whitehead. *Method in Ministry: Theological Reflection and Christian Ministry.* Minneapolis: Winston-Seabury, 1981.

———. *Seasons of Strength: New Visions of Adult Christian Maturing.* Garden City, N.Y.: Doubleday Image, 1986.

Wink, Walter. *Naming the Powers: The Language of Power in the New Testament.* Philadelphia: Fortress Press, 1984.

Worgul, George. *From Magic to Metaphor.* New York: Paulist Press, 1980.

INDEX

ABOUT THE AUTHORS

JAMES D. WHITEHEAD is a pastoral theologian and historian of religion. He holds the doctorate from Harvard University, with a concentration in Chinese religions. His professional interests include issues of contemporary spirituality and theological method in ministry.

EVELYN EATON WHITEHEAD is a developmental psychologist, with the doctorate from the University of Chicago. She writes and lectures on questions of adult development, aging and the analysis of community and parish life.

The Whiteheads are authors of *Christian Life Patterns,* a selection of the Catholic Book Club, now available in Doubleday Image Edition. Their book *Marrying Well: Stages on the Journey of Christian Marriage,* also available in Doubleday Image Edition, was a selection of the Religious Book Club. Their other books include *Method in Ministry, Community of Faith,* and *Seasons of Strength.*

In 1978 they established Whitehead Associates, through which they serve as consultants in education and ministry. They are members of the associate faculty of the Institute of Pastoral Studies at Loyola University in Chicago. The Whiteheads currently make their home in South Bend, Indiana.